T0271604

"*Writing the Wrongs* is a crucial resource that ac rigor with compassionate insight. It offers those a structured yet personal path to healing and innovative use of writing as therapy provides individuals to reclaim their narrative and begin the journey to recovery."

—Bill Edmonds, LTC (Ret) Army Special Forces, author of *God Is Not Here*

"*Writing the Wrongs* is an intelligent and well-thought-out guide to going inside and journaling both one's pain and one's release. Anyone who takes the time to engage with the book and do the work will find help for their suffering."

—Fred Luskin, PhD, author of *Forgive for Good*, director of the Stanford Forgiveness Project, and affiliate faculty member of the Greater Good Science Center at UC Berkeley

"This is no mere journal—it's an embodied journey of reckoning and reconnection, making us feel held in our darkest moments. Whether you're a trauma survivor, health-care worker, veteran, or struggling with a crisis of conscience, *Writing the Wrongs* will be a treasured companion and a beacon of hope for transforming moral anguish into post-traumatic growth. Weaving cutting-edge neuroscience with ancient wisdom, DeMarco's groundbreaking approach is medicine for our times."

—Albert Wong, PhD, director of the Trauma Certificate Program at Somatopia, and author of *The Healing Trauma Workbook*

"In a world experiencing a dearth of soul, DeMarco's compassionate approach to moral injury is a poetic answer to tending the personal wounds of the individual self. *Writing the Wrongs* is a beautiful offering for anyone struggling with the impact of soul wounding or looking to rewrite the narrative of their life."

—Valeria McCarroll, PhD, LMFT, faculty at the California Institute of Integral Studies, psychedelic educator/consultant, writer, and speaker

"DeMarco offers a science-based GPS to navigate the adverse terrain of moral injury and trauma—which strikes a particular chord with combat veterans like me. The writing prompts are meticulously crafted and aimed at fostering awareness, acknowledging the past, reshaping the present, and envisioning a hopeful future. DeMarco's work is set apart by her profound insights and compassion, and her astute identification of moral trauma as 'soul wounds.'"

—Troy Arce, DACM, LAc, career pararescueman and combat rescue officer, and veteran community care provider

"Thoughtful and reassuring, *Writing the Wrongs* brings a valuable new perspective to how writing can resolve trauma by honoring and engaging the imagination, while envisioning and, importantly, compassionately re-visioning the lives people want for themselves."

—Cindy Shearer, DA, professor and program chair of the MFA in interdisciplinary arts and writing, and PhD in psychology programs at the California Institute of Integral Studies (CIIS)

"*Writing the Wrongs* offers an insightful and pragmatic approach to the often-ignored trauma of moral injury. Through reflective writing and engaged imagination, these pages offer a gentle guide to recovery and self-discovery. It is a gift and a resource to those seeking to rebuild their inner world and find a deeper sense of wholeness."

—Jonathan Erickson, PhD, MFA, author of *Imagination in the Western Psyche*, faculty at CIIS, and communication and narrative coach

"*Writing the Wrongs* helps readers identify their own moral injuries and offers a comprehensive guide to independently work through, and ultimately conquer, their deepest, most personal wounds. It will immensely benefit anyone seeking healing from 'soul wounds,' especially our nation's most elite warriors, who are suffering immensely from the destructive impacts of operator syndrome and moral injury, as well as their families."

—Jennifer E. Byrne, BS, MS, OTD, OTR/L, vice president and cofounder at Shields & Stripes, and CEO at 5by5 Performance Therapy

New Harbinger Journals for Change

Research shows that journaling has a universally positive effect on mental health. But in the midst of life's difficulties—such as stress, anxiety, depression, relationship problems, parenting challenges, or even obsessive or negative thoughts—where do you begin? New Harbinger *Journals for Change* combine evidence-based psychology with proven-effective guided journaling techniques to help you make lasting personal change—one page at a time. Written by renowned mental health and wellness experts, *Journals for Change* provide a creative and safe space to process difficult emotions, work through challenges, reflect on what matters, and set intentions for the future.

Since 1973, New Harbinger has published practical, user-friendly self-help books and workbooks to help readers make positive change. Our *Journals for Change* offer the same powerfully effective tools—without ever *feeling* like therapy. If you're committed to improving your mental health, these easy-to-use guided journals can help you take small, actionable steps toward lasting well-being.

For a complete list of journals in our *Journals for Change* series, visit newharbinger.com.

Writing

the

Wrongs

A Guided Journal
for Healing Moral Injury

Michele DeMarco, PhD

New Harbinger Publications, Inc.

Publisher's Note

This publication is designed to provide accurate and authoritative information in regard to the subject matter covered. It is sold with the understanding that the publisher is not engaged in rendering psychological, financial, legal, or other professional services. If expert assistance or counseling is needed, the services of a competent professional should be sought.

Printed in the United States of America

26   25   24

10   9   8   7   6   5   4   3   2   1   First Printing

You don't always have control over the events in life,
but the script you live by is yours to write—
and write it you must, as only you can.

(THIS JOURNAL BELONGS TO)

(DATE STARTED / DATE COMPLETE)

For Becca, whose strength, moral integrity and resilience inspires me daily and shines as the strongest beacon.

Contents

*Memory is a powerful tool;
when it speaks, it tells a
story—and this account
often has more influence
than historical fact.*

Writing About Trauma

For many people, it isn't easy to talk about a traumatic experience like *moral injury* or *moral distress*, which is one reason why writing can be beneficial. It allows you to record your deeper thoughts and feelings about challenging events in a safe and private manner. Still, working through trauma does require careful and intentional engagement with memories that may be triggering.

This journal is inspired by *embodied disclosure therapy* (EDT; DeMarco, 2022), a science-backed approach to moral injury I developed that is safe and well-researched. The original protocol requires that the writing be done with a therapist. In this journal, you may be working alone. I have worked hard to adapt my research so that you can move through the process on your own; however, writing is a type of exposure, which may bring up difficult emotions and sensations. While the following exercises were purposefully designed to minimize discomfort, it is always beneficial to stay attentive to how you're feeling.

For urgent help from a trained professional:

- All emergencies: Dial 911
- SAMHSA National Helpline: 1-800-622-HELP (4357)
- National Suicide Prevention Lifeline: 1-800-273-TALK (8255)
- Crisis Text Line: Text HOME to 741741

This journal is not psychotherapy nor a replacement for psychotherapy with a licensed professional. You are encouraged to seek out therapy if you are interested. This journal can also be used in your therapeutic work.

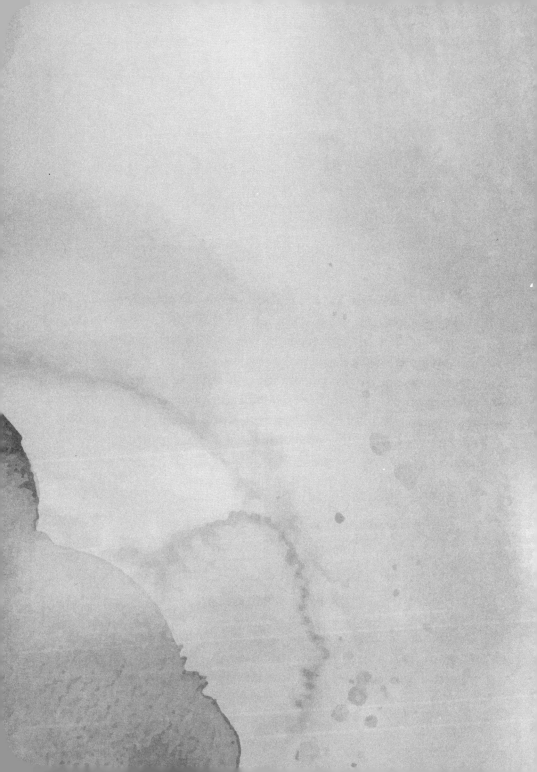

Welcome, I'm glad you're here...

I'm Dr. Michele DeMarco, and I've spent the last two decades on a "souljourn," studying trauma generally, moral injury and moral distress specifically, and resilience. "Soul wounds," as they are commonly known, happen when our core values, beliefs, or bonds are violated or compromised. And they hurt because they cut to the *very things that define us*. Soul wounds can be heavy burdens to bear. But you've come to the right place.

I developed this journal for you—to help you thrive through some of the most painful experiences of your life. In it, you will better understand what a soul wound is, how it lives inside you, how that shapes the stories you tell yourself, and how that affects your relationships with others and the world. If you're curious about my background and why you can trust me, you can read my whole story at micheledemarco.com.

Healing from moral trauma and moral adversity requires engaging the effects that may be negatively influencing your feelings, thoughts, and beliefs and contributing to injury narratives. The good news is that it can be done with or without a therapist. Not everyone has access to specialized treatment, or treatment at all, and many cannot afford it.

Seeking help for moral trauma or moral adversity is a bold and courageous move; it's also a mark of strength and resilience. Opening this book shows your desire for a better and more meaningful future. Turning the pages, as you work through the process, is a testament to that commitment.

Honoring pain, reconciling difficult truths, transforming ways of thinking and being, and restoring moral integrity starts here.

I am honored to be part of your journey.

Wishing you renewed peace and wellness.
With gratitude for your interest and trust.

If your core moral foundation was violated in a high-stakes situation, you may have experienced moral trauma.

Introduction

Moral trauma, especially moral injury and moral distress, is one of the most important but little-known areas of trauma and healing today. And it's different from depression, anxiety, feelings of burnout or defeat, and even traditionally expressed *post-traumatic stress disorder* (PTSD).

Moral injury happens when your core moral foundations are violated in high-stakes situations. This violation recasts the way you see yourself, others, and the world, and can cause changes in behavior that signal a loss of trust, connection, self-worth, and meaning.

Violations can happen from actions you took (such as killing or harming a person, whether it was intentional, unintentional, or unavoidable); actions you witnessed, including betrayal (like abuse, violence, infidelity, discrimination, or being wrongly accused); being forced to act against your will or better judgment (like abandoning or neglecting someone or lying, cheating, or falsifying information because a person in authority commanded you to); and actions that couldn't be taken to prevent a bad situation from happening (such as natural disasters, accidents, suicide, and medical injury or illness).

Struggling with moral trauma or moral adversity often involves a range of emotions like shame, guilt, anger, disgust, contempt, resentment, despair, grief, remorse, worthlessness, hopelessness, helplessness, powerlessness, alienation, self-loathing, and hate. Sometimes, after a while, you might even stop feeling anything at all.

Depending on the type of violation, it's common to lose trust in yourself, others, God, and/or the world. You might see yourself as bad, evil, weak, a monster, or unworthy—or you might see others that way. Perhaps the world no longer makes sense or now seems unsafe and unfamiliar. Maybe you've lost faith or have trouble forgiving, expressing compassion, or relating to and connecting with others.

With moral trauma, particularly moral injury, relationship challenges often erupt, like avoiding intimacy, self-isolating, and lashing out at the littlest provocation. Because the "story" of moral injury is often too painful to share, you may conclude others couldn't understand, wouldn't understand, or would judge and so you "swallow the awful" and live in self-segregating silence. It's also not uncommon to try to hide your pain with alcohol or drugs, or by engaging in risky and self-sabotaging behavior. Suicidal thoughts are also not uncommon.

One of the most common things I hear when I discuss moral injury is, "So *that's* what it's called!" While the field of moral trauma is gaining attention, many people don't know its name, let alone its painful effects, often confusing their

Moral Injury	BOTH	PTSD
Relational: Threat to existential safety, to the core-connected self	Reminders	Physical: Threat to bodily safety
	Intrusive thoughts	
	Sleep issues	Concern for physical survival
Loss of trust or faith	Suicidality/Suicide risk	Re-experiencing
Rumination	Insomnia	
	Anxiety	Avoidance: Prevent flashback
Avoidance: Protect others from you or protect yourself from others	Depression	Shame: Not being able to "handle" your responses
	Dissociation	
	Nightmares	Role: Recipient or witness
Shame: For what you did, were forced to do, or couldn't prevent	Risky behavior	"Startle" reflex
	Anti-socialization	
	Fatalism	More sympathetically oriented
Role: Recipient, witness, or perpetrator	Substance abuse	
	Anger, disgust	
"Gag" or "gut" reflex	Shame	
More parasympathetically oriented		

anguish with PTSD. While there are similarities, there are also important differences. Here is a chart with a few.

Moral distress, related to moral injury, can happen when institutional or systemic barriers prevent you from acting with integrity, particularly when it comes to fundamental moral principles and ethical responsibilities. At times, actions deemed to be ethical are different from the ones a person would naturally choose if otherwise available.

Moral distress affects professions, such as healthcare workers, social service providers, teachers, law enforcement, the military, emergency service providers, lawyers, journalists, and politicians, among others. In our day-to-day lives, this type of suffering can take a serious toll on beliefs, relationships, and affiliations. In its extreme form, it can result in "otherizing."

Powerlessness, particularly, is at the heart of moral distress. It is the feeling of having had to, or must seriously, compromise yourself or something you hold dear due to external forces seemingly beyond your control. It is also the sense that others don't grasp a moral significance or moral imperative that is clear to you. Moral distress is what results from repeatedly not having your values respected, either individually or collectively.

If you have moral distress, you may feel muzzled, restricted, devalued, unheard, or dismissed. You might easily become fueled by anger, disgust, fear, and frustration. Over time, these emotions can fill you with anxiety, depletion, or depression. A sense of being fragmented can set in, leaving you to question who you or others are at the core and what the world is, generally, like moral injury. Research (Ruston, 2017) shows that moral distress has long-term consequences, such as burnout, exhaustion, numbness, disconnection, and diminished moral sensitivity (also called "compassion fatigue").

The damaging effects of moral distress aren't limited to you, who is primarily carrying the burden. Others you interact with can also be negatively impacted due to changes in your attitudes or actions toward them.

❧ Path to Healing Moral Injury ❧

Three decades ago, it was thought that the secret to healing from trauma was for a person to share their own "traumatic secrets" (or story) with a trusted and validating witness. What we've learned in that time is that forced sharing of details often makes the traumatic experience worse, not better. Many people think they can—or should be able to—simply "think" their way out of feeling the intense, crushing, and often confusing reactions that plague them, but advances in neuroscience, moral emotions, and somatic psychology tell us otherwise. In short, trauma changes our brain and body—it causes our "rational" thinking-mind that plans, remembers, keeps us connected, maintains perspective, and processes clearly to automatically shut down, interpreting a threat. This kicks older areas of the brain like the limbic system into high gear that have us fighting, fleeing, freezing, or shutting down entirely.

The traumatized brain goes offline each time you are triggered by a sight, sound, smell, taste, touch, or memory, sending messages of fear, distrust, and disconnection coursing through your body.

Exposure therapies, which expose you to trauma triggers in a therapeutic setting, have proven effective for PTSD, but less so for soul wounds, like moral injury and moral distress. *Embodied disclosure therapy* (EDT; DeMarco, 2022) and the *Imaginal Writing* program here were intentionally designed to "expose" you to these triggers through the process of writing while also giving you real-time prompts and practices that allow your brain and body to feel safe and the greatest amount of reflection, meaning-making, and connection—all of which are essential for healing soul wounds.

The Imaginal Writing Program

The desire to record the most challenging or intimate details of life is as old as handwriting itself. It wasn't until the late 1980s that James Pennebaker and his colleagues (1986) discovered that expressing deeper thoughts and feelings through writing can result in significant health benefits. Since then, "writing to heal" has received meaningful attention, both in research and practice with various approaches emerging.

One approach, which I developed, is *Imaginal Writing*. It is a way of engaging the imagination to safely and creatively explore the values, beliefs, and experiences that may be contributing to your moral pain and holding you back. Imaginal Writing starts from the premise that the imagination is a portal to the deepest parts of us, where integrity and wholeness lie, and that the work of identity reconstruction—or what I call *Soul Remaking*—is enhanced by examining the ways symptoms and symbolism collide and influence how we see and relate to ourselves, others, and the world. I describe the "soul" generally as the deepest part of you where integrity lies.

Imaginal Writing also affirms that, like love and joy, moral violations (including betrayal) serve your soul at the very moment they seem to be a tragedy. The pain you feel—such as shame, guilt, disgust, despair, disillusionment, emptiness, and isolation—is not an indicator of a soul in tatters and beyond repair. It's simply another expression of your soul's voice and values calling out to be heard.

Imaginal Writing allows you to engage slowly with what is deepest inside you and what is most important for you. The goal is not to create a work of art. Rather, it is to engage with your imagination, particularly your moral imagination, and sensory experience over time. This pacing allows you to rediscover trust, confidence, wisdom, energy, and connection with the people and things that matter most—including yourself.

The guiding principle of Imaginal Writing is to become present to your moral pain, not by denying the pain; instead, by allowing it to be felt; recording the pain honestly, without hypocrisy, dishonesty, sentimentality, or idealization; and recounting the pain directly. In doing so, new understandings about the pain are revealed, as are opportunities to transform that pain into empowerment and purpose.

Imaginal Writing uniquely leverages grounding and somatic exercises that are essential to the journaling process. More on that soon.

Essential Preparation:
What to Expect and How to Plan

Engaging moral pain or soul wounds takes some heart-centered work, which doesn't always come easily. As with any pain or injury, the key to healing lies in understanding and addressing its cause. In the case of moral pain or injury, understanding the context—that is, the situation surrounding the experience that violated your core values, beliefs, or identity—the key players, the stakes, and both the type and the degree of harm are essential for the healing process.

Like many people, you may not know how to do so in a way that doesn't make you feel vulnerable, outraged, or overwhelmed. The following grounding practices and other somatic techniques can minimize discomfort when you integrate them into the writing process.

⤬ Getting into an Embodied State ⤬

Getting into an embodied state is helpful before diving into each writing prompt. Essentially, an embodied state is a felt awareness of the entire body—all the tactile sensations that flicker and shift beneath your skin and whisper words in a language all their own to affect how you feel and what you think. It's a sensory awareness that helps you to feel open yet grounded.

Centering practices are good ways into an embodied state. "Centering" refers to being in a relaxed and focused state. It's a way to bring calm to your emotions, which is especially helpful when you're feeling a strong emotion that often results in the wake of moral pain. At the start of each part of this journal, a different centering practice is provided. If you have a preferred one, feel free to use it.

ぐ Engaging Difficult Emotions ぐ

As I mentioned, writing about traumatic experiences, including moral injury and moral distress, can cause difficult or strong emotions to bubble up. While these emotions don't feel great, they're not something to fear or avoid. Emotions are inherently neither good nor bad; they're simply messengers. They tell you what's working and what isn't, what's missing, and what you need more of, among other things. In this way, each has an important function.

The key to emotionally caring for yourself lies in recognizing what you are sensing in a moment, gauging its purpose for a given situation, and choosing to hold onto it or let it go. Doing so requires being in touch with your internal landscape. Unfortunately, this is not something that comes naturally, especially to adults, nor is it something typically taught to kids, like the ABCs. It also becomes harder to do when you've experienced trauma because traumatic experiences run roughshod over the body, bringing you to the edge of your "window of tolerance," the optimal arousal level that allows emotions to ebb and flow.

Part of getting at the emotional truth of your morally distressing experience is understanding the somatic (body) story as much as the cognitive (mind) one. This requires bringing awareness to the inner "murky places," ripe with sensations, emotions, and feelings. If you're familiar with the story of Goldilocks, Goldilocks sampled three types of porridge and found she preferred the porridge that was "just right," not too hot and not too cold. Similarly, the key to emotional learning and soulful healing is finding the right amount of arousal to bring into your system. It's like turning the handles on a faucet: too much and you get splattered or soaked; too little and you can't get the job of washing done.

The word "titrate" is often used to describe how much emotional "flow" you let come into your system's internal reservoir. To titrate your experience is to keep yourself in an intentional place of choice and safety by opening and closing the tap on your emotions. It's a process that slows down your internal response—emotional, cognitive, and physiological—so that you can more effectively process incoming information. It's a skill that you can practice as you engage the prompts in this journal.

⤳ Distress Tolerance Techniques ⤳

There may be moments during writing when you do feel activated by strong or uncomfortable emotions, feelings, or sensations. First, know that this is normal, so don't beat yourself up about it. Second, the following distress tolerance techniques can be used during writing to pause and restore calm. They have been adapted from science-backed therapies that help to regulate strong emotions.

For when you're feeling anxious, agitated, or stressed:

Diaphragmatic or "Belly" Breathing

Diaphragmatic breathing means that when you inhale, your belly expands outward. When you exhale, your belly should cave in. The more your belly expands and caves in, the deeper you're breathing—which is what you want. This method is quick and can be practiced anywhere. The key is to slow your breath from the typical 10 to14 breaths per minute to 5 to 7 breaths per minute. An easy way to do this is by inhaling for a count of 5, holding it briefly, and exhaling for a count of 10. While it's nice to lie down, this practice can be done in any position.

Grounding Techniques

Grounding (or "earthing" as it is sometimes called) is a way to focus on what is physically happening to you, whether in your body or your surroundings.

It's a technique that breaks the cycle of hyperarousal—that is, being overly agitated—by bringing you into the present and out of fixating on the past or future. One technique for grounding is *5–4–3–2–1*. To begin, notice your surroundings. Inhale and exhale, slowly and big. Then name 5 things you can see around you (in your space, out the window). Name 4 things you can feel (warmth of your skin, your feet against the floor, the table in front of you), 3 things you can hear (cars on the road, birds in the trees, a humming in the ceiling vent), and 2 things you can smell (take a deep breath in). Finally, name 1 good thing about yourself.

For when you're feeling down, depressed, despair, or dissociated (that is, shutdown or checked out):

The Squeeze Ball

Paced resistance can help to slowly and safely bring energy back into your body. Get a palm-sized ball (a tennis ball or small yoga ball, even your dog's rubber ball can work) and slowly, evenly squeeze and release it. You can also massage it. As you do, bring awareness to your fingers. Focus on the tension and release of that tension. Continue for a minute or two.

Bounce

Otherwise known as "rebounding," bouncing increases blood flow to your brain and muscles, releasing endorphins, the feel-good chemicals in your brain, to boost your mood while detoxifying your system. Even a few minutes of bouncing can help to pull you out of feeling blue.

⤳ What To Expect and How To Plan ⤳

This guided journal is structured to support your writing about your experience of moral pain. I advise you to use imagery, visualization, analogy, and metaphor and make the writing intimate and personal. Please don't worry about grammar, spelling, or page count during writing. Also, you needn't worry about the quality of the writing, or the outcome or audience (this writing is only for you). After writing, you'll have the opportunity to reflect on how the experience was for you and to rate your experience on a scale from 0 to 10 (more on that below) so you can track your progress.

Here are some things to help you prepare:

Writing Time

There is no schedule for writing; however, consistency and a dedicated time to write help make the process more powerful and the healing more sustainable. Schedule between 20 to 30 minutes to devote to your writing session. (If you would like to write longer, by all means do.) You'll spend the first 2 to 3 minutes getting settled and grounded, the next chunk writing in response to the prompts, and the final 2 to 3 minutes checking in on how the writing session went.

It's helpful to schedule your writing session just as you would any other appointment—including marking it in your calendar.

Writing Space

The best, most insightful, and most productive writing comes when you have a comfortable, safe, and private space for yourself. Make sure your space is free of distractions; this means no cell phone, computer, iNotebook, or other digital devices; and no TV, noises, people, or objects that could draw your attention away from your writing.

Writing for Yourself

I suggest writing in the first person (using "I" statements such as, "It was Monday when I left the house for work"). Writing in the first person makes the story more intimate, which can help you really get at what the experience of moral integrity is for you.

Write at a slow to moderate pace. Use imagery, visualization, analogy, and metaphor to make the experience come to life. Also, make the writing intimate and personal: identify people, conversations, ideas, objects, or behaviors that are contributing to feelings of moral integrity.

Be sure to include emotions, feelings, and inner sensations (like fluid or shallow breathing, a calm or racing heartbeat, relaxed or tensed muscles, or an easy or stiff posture) that you experience. For example, "I had a lump in my throat and felt sick when I realized what was happening, but as soon as I spoke up against it, the sickness went away, and I suddenly felt warm and whole." It's also helpful to pause occasionally and tune into how you're feeling in the present and link those experiences to current inner body sensations, like, "In that moment, I felt scared, like my world might never be the same, but now as I write this, I feel my chest surge with pride at how I said what I said." Allow these positive feelings to wash over you for a few moments, then return to writing. If at any time you feel agitated or overwhelmed, pause and use one of the distress tolerance techniques mentioned above to help restore calm.

Writing, by nature, is a type of exposure. You may afterward experience images, thoughts, feelings, and sensations that you wrote about. This is perfectly natural, and they should not be pushed away. If at any time you do feel distressed, try using the grounding exercises or distress tolerance techniques included in this journal to help restore calm.

⤳ Getting Ready and What to Remember ⤳

The writing prompts vary in length; some have brief introductions or exercises to begin. Each writing prompt should be read through first in its entirety and then followed as instructed. Writing sessions begin with a grounding exercise to get you in the necessary embodied state to engage the writing prompts. It's also helpful to remember:

- **Don't rush the process.** Take whatever time you need to really delve into that prompt in a way that sets you up for success. Drop in when you can be fully present to it and drop out when it becomes too much. The only schedule you are on is your own.

- **Queue up trusted others.** You may want to discuss new insights and experiences with someone else in addition to processing them yourself. Good support is essential, so be sure to reach out to your inner circle.

- **Share the process.** If someone else you know is going through a similar experience with moral pain, it can be helpful to chat about each of your progress, challenges, or questions.

- **Don't jump ahead to other prompts.** Do them in the order they're presented.

At the conclusion of each session, there is also an optional grounding exercise. If you are in counseling or treatment, you may wish to consult your therapist or other professional prior to beginning the process.

After writing, you will check in on how you're feeling using two scales: one for how distressed you're feeling, and another for how open and available to others/life you feel. For each, you'll rate your feelings from 0 (not at all) to 10 (extremely). These ratings will give you a quick way to measure change over the course of the program.

You now have everything you need to engage the writing journey and get on the path to healing, hope, and wholeness.

WRITING
PROMPTS

High or low, right or wrong,
it's all true.

PART 1

Grounding in Awareness

The writing prompts in Grounding in Awareness are designed to help you better understand and engage your moral pain, as well as your moral strengths and areas for growth. You'll be asked to focus on the sensations, emotions, feelings, and postures that arise when writing about your painful experience. These kinds of inner physical stirrings can influence how you think and feel, which can then shape the story you tell and live by. Each prompt involves facilitating states of arousal and calm so that you can learn to titrate your emotions and stay in your rational, clear-eyed, meaning-making mind.

Grounding in Awareness invites you to awaken your moral core and become deeply familiar with your moral compass. Often, we think we know our morals, values, guiding principles, and sacred beliefs; moreover, where the line is which crosses them—that is, until a painful experience pulls the rug out from beneath us and calls everything into question. Grounding in Awareness helps you to understand what, specifically, moral integrity looks like for you and identify your core wound and what is necessary to heal and move forward with a whole soul once again.

CENTERING EXERCISE

CELLULAR BREATHING

When we're nervous or hyper-focused, we hold our breath. When we're overstimulated, it's difficult to catch our breath. When we try to suppress tears or stifle a strong emotion, our breath becomes weak or irregular. Reminding yourself to breathe—*and* breathe deeply—can help you to stay calm, focused, and connected.

Cellular breathing focuses on the pure sensations of natural breath.

1. Start by sitting comfortably in a chair or lying flat on the ground. Place your right hand over your heart and your left hand on your belly.

2. Notice the places where your body is touching the earth (or ground). Let these places sink downward.

3. In the stillness, start to notice the rhythm of your breath. Inhale, feel the lungs fill. Exhale, feel the lungs empty.

4. Notice what happens in your body when you focus on your hands— the weight, the temperature, sensations throughout your body, changes in breathing.

5. Now, focus on the hand on your belly. Feel it rise on the exhale and lower on the inhale. Keep doing this and notice what's happening. Maybe the breath feels cool on the way in and warm on the way out, or that your heart has space around it.

6. Imagine a wave cresting and falling—bringing in fresh, clean air, restoring and replenishing the toxins that are taken out when the wave falls.

When you're ready, start to make some small movements. Take a moment, bring your attention back to your surroundings, turn your attention to the prompt, and begin to write.

❧ PROMPT 1 ❧

Awakening Your Core Integrity

Write about an experience when you acted with moral integrity. That is, when you did something that made you feel whole, strong, safe, proud, confident, authentic, and at peace. Maybe you stood up for something or someone you believed in strongly or followed through on an important promise you made. Maybe you refrained from sharing important secrets or held a confidence despite meaningful pressure or you told the truth even though it was hard or against your best interests. Maybe you admitted you were wrong.

When you're ready, pick up your pen and get writing.

_____

_____

_____

_____

_____

_____

_____

_____

❧ Post-Writing Check-In ☙

Take a few moments to sit quietly without looking at what you wrote to transition to the present. Taking a few deep and quiet breaths can help. Mark how you're feeling in this moment on the scales below and jot down any thoughts that arise.

How distressed are you feeling in this moment?	How connected to others and life are you feeling in this moment?
(none) 0 1 2 3 4 5 6 7 8 9 10 (extremely)	(none) 0 1 2 3 4 5 6 7 8 9 10 (extremely)

How did the writing feel?

_____

_____

_____

_____

What was challenging about it?

_____

_____

_____

What did you find inspiring or helpful, with any soulful moments of reconnection?

_____

_____

_____

_____

_____

What insights or messages from the writing process can you carry with you?

_____

_____

_____

_____

_____

Writing, by nature, is a type of exposure experience. Even when you're recounting a positive experience, you may afterward experience images, thoughts, feelings, and sensations that you wrote about. This is perfectly natural, and they should not be pushed away.

❧ PROMPT 2 ❧

Messages in Pain

Take a few minutes to get comfortable—feel the chair holding you, the floor beneath you, the sights and sounds around you, and the air moving through you. Sit with this as you consider the moral pain that urged you to pick up this guided journal. Perhaps it's the result of actions you took that violated your core values or sacred beliefs, or the actions that another took. Maybe you were betrayed by someone meaningful or forced to do something against your will or better judgment. Maybe you couldn't prevent something bad from happening or repeatedly compromise yourself and what you hold dear to do your job or function in a group, organization, or even family. Perhaps it's a combination of these things.

Now, consider how this is affecting you—the feelings and emotions that bubble up (or explode), the "crazy" thoughts that seize your mind and won't let go, or how you've acted (or didn't act, even shutdown) since this experience. The list below offers common effects. It's helpful to circle those that are especially resonant.

Shame	Hopelessness	Can't feel pleasure
Guilt	Powerlessness	Relationship problems
Contempt	Loss of trust/faith	
Anger	Loss of meaning	Blame/ Condemnation
Disgust	Intrusive thoughts	Inability to forgive
Anxiety	Apathy	Less empathy
Depression	Alienation	Risky behavior
Resentment	Isolation	Substance abuse
Despair	Numbing/ Shutdown	Self-harm
Grief	Queasiness	Suicidal thoughts
Worthlessness		

When you're ready, begin writing. This prompt has three parts. It can be done in one or more writing sessions.

#1: PAINFUL VOICES

Imagine your moral pain is a character that can speak. What kind of voice does it have? Ask your pain, "Who are you?" "Why are you here?" "What are you trying to tell me?" Reflect on, then record, what it's like to hear your pain speak to you. Notice how the words make you feel, for instance, angry, relieved. Perhaps you have a racing heart, a heavy heart, tense muscles, are breathing fast, and the like. If at any time you start to feel distressed or overwhelmed, take a few deep breaths and say to yourself, "I'm doing well. Just try to stay with the feeling a bit more." Consider what messages those sensations are carrying about your experience of moral injury or moral distress.

_____

_____

_____

_____

_____

_____

_____

_____

_____

#2: METAPHORS OF MEANING

Imagine a metaphor for your moral pain or soul wound. What images do you see? What senses can you feel? What do you hear from the metaphor's voice? Reflect on, then record, what it feels like to sit in the presence of that metaphor. Notice which emotions bubble up. Consider what messages those feelings and sensations carry about your experience of moral injury or moral distress.

#3: PAIN COME TO LIFE

Imagine your worst symptom has come to life. Maybe that's the feeling of shame, guilt, anger, disgust, despair, grief, worthlessness, alienation, isolation, or the like. What would it look or sound like? How would it act? What would it be trying to tell you? What does it need you to know?

❧ Post-Writing Check-In ❧

Take a few moments to sit quietly without looking at what you wrote to transition to the present. Taking a few deep and quiet breaths can help. Mark how you're feeling in this moment on the scales below and jot down any thoughts that arise.

How distressed are you feeling in this moment?	How connected to others and life are you feeling in this moment?
(none) 0 1 2 3 4 5 6 7 8 9 10 (extremely)	(none) 0 1 2 3 4 5 6 7 8 9 10 (extremely)

How did the writing feel?

_____

_____

_____

_____

What was challenging about it?

_____

_____

_____

What did you find inspiring or helpful with any soulful moments of reconnection?

❧ PROMPT 3 ❧

Identifying Desire

This prompt has six parts. It can be done in one or more writing sessions.

Imagine the words *meaning, purpose, value, connection, resilience,* and *transcendence.* Together, they are what's been called the Six Fundamental Human Desires (DeMarco, 2023) that all human beings long for in their lives. Take each word separately and recount how your moral pain or wound has directly affected your ability to satisfy each desire. Here are some prompts:

#1: MEANING

What is now gone that was once especially important to you? What beliefs have been called into question that once helped you to make sense of yourself, others, and the world? (For example, trust, companionship, the belief that you are invincible.) Are there any that have become stronger or weaker?

_____

_____

_____

_____

_____

_____

#2: PURPOSE

What, if any, pathways to the future seem closed off because of this pain or wound? What detours will you need to take to move forward?

_____

_____

_____

_____

_____

_____

_____

_____

_____

_____

_____

_____

_____

_____

_____

#3: VALUE

How has your pain or wound distracted you from what matters most in your life? What mattered most in your life before? Does it still? What was your "ultimate concern"—the unifying focus of your life? How has this been affected by what's happened?

#4: CONNECTION

What relationships have changed because of this violation or soul wound? What makes that so? What specifically have you done (or failed to do) to affect them?

#5: RESILIENCE

How specifically has this violation or soul wound weakened you or made you smaller? What resources are you no longer leveraging? What negative thoughts are holding you back?

#6: TRANSCENDENCE

How, where, and with what frequency did you use to find wonder and awe, or if you like, God or a Higher Power? How has this changed since this violation or soul wound? In what ways? What makes that so?

ꙮ Post-Writing Check-In ꙮ

Take a few moments to sit quietly without looking at what you wrote to transition to the present. Taking a few deep and quiet breaths can help. Mark how you're feeling in this moment on the scales below and jot down any thoughts that arise.

How distressed are you feeling in this moment?	How connected to others and life are you feeling in this moment?
(none) 0 1 2 3 4 5 6 7 8 9 10 (extremely)	(none) 0 1 2 3 4 5 6 7 8 9 10 (extremely)

How did the writing feel?

_____

_____

_____

_____

_____

What was challenging about it?

_____

_____

_____

What did you find inspiring or helpful with any soulful moments of reconnection?

✧ PROMPT 4 ✧

Identifying Your Moral Harm

Write the story of your morally painful experience. If you have more than one, choose an experience that continues to weigh particularly heavy. Recount the experience from a place of wholeness prior to the events that caused the moral pain. It can be helpful to include what your strengths, successes, desires, or expectations were ahead of the experience. For instance, "I've always been a person who cares deeply about loyalty—I give it and I expect it, but when..." Then, as if watching a movie in slow motion, take the story to the events that led to the harm.

Be sure to include the "unruly parts" or "hot spots" (that is those that may have caused a sense of anger, fear, shame, guilt, disgust, anxiety, overwhelm, or no longer being in control of the situation or outcome)—but only write about them in 45 to 60 second intervals; doing so will make the writing easier. After the 45 to 60 seconds, pause and tune in to the present moment, linking these unruly parts to real-time inner body sensations (for instance, heavy breathing, a racing heart, tense muscles, a turning stomach, trembling or shaking, or a change in your body's temperature).

If these unruly parts cause anxiety or other intense emotions, pause, and bring calm by taking slow, deep breaths, bringing attention to your surroundings or placing a hand over the area of your body that has experienced the shift in discomfort. Breathe deeply, allowing the sensation to move through you and out. You can also use one of the distress tolerance techniques.

When you're ready, return to writing—and if you feel these intense feelings again, simply repeat the steps above as necessary until the end of the writing session.

⌒ Post-Writing Check-In ⌒

Take a few moments to sit quietly without looking at what you wrote to transition to the present. Taking a few deep and quiet breaths can help. Mark how you're feeling in this moment on the scales below and jot down any thoughts that arise.

How distressed are you feeling in this moment?	How connected to others and life are you feeling in this moment?
(none) 0 1 2 3 4 5 6 7 8 9 10 (extremely)	(none) 0 1 2 3 4 5 6 7 8 9 10 (extremely)

How did the writing feel?

_____

_____

_____

_____

What was challenging about it?

_____

_____

_____

What did you find inspiring or helpful with any soulful moments of reconnection?

∽ PROMPT 5 ∾

Identifying Your Core Wound

Continue writing about the same morally painful experience. This time, choose one part of the story that carries the deepest core wound. Core wounds can be things that are now gone that were once especially important; beliefs that have been called into question that once helped you to make sense of the world; pathways to the future that seem closed off as a result of this experience; how this experience has distracted you from what matters most in your life; specific relationships that have changed as a result of this experience; and how specifically this experience has weakened you or made you smaller.

Write slowly, deliberately, and with "benevolent honesty," that is a kindness and gentleness toward yourself in the recounting, as if each word carries essential, even sacred, meaning. As you consider each response, ask yourself what's going on inside and slowly drop into those sensations, rather than push them away, noticing the images, thoughts, and messages that arise.

Write without distraction about how this core wound has changed your view of yourself, others, and the world.

∽ Post-Writing Check-In ∽

Take a few moments to sit quietly without looking at what you wrote to transition to the present. Taking a few deep and quiet breaths can help. Mark how you're feeling in this moment on the scales below and jot down any thoughts that arise.

How distressed are you feeling in this moment?	How connected to others and life are you feeling in this moment?
(none) 0 1 2 3 4 5 6 7 8 9 10 (extremely)	(none) 0 1 2 3 4 5 6 7 8 9 10 (extremely)

How did the writing feel?

_____

_____

_____

_____

_____

What was challenging about it?

_____

_____

_____

What did you find inspiring or helpful with any soulful moments of reconnection?

CONCLUDING EXERCISE

WHEN YOU FELT MOST LIKE YOURSELF

This exercise is adapted from Peter Levine's (2008) therapeutic approach, Somatic Experiencing.

Find a quiet place, either sitting or lying down. Close your eyes and take a moment to notice your overall experience. Then, recall a time in the last few days when you felt most like yourself. Maybe you felt closer to your true or authentic self, or the self you desire to be or would like to be more of the time. Perhaps you felt more alive or joyful than anxious or sad. Perhaps something you experienced gave you a deep sense of meaning and purpose.

Recall this time in a detailed way—as though it is happening now. Notice what happens inside your body in *this* moment. Especially notice your five senses. Don't judge what occurs. Just notice it. Shift back and forth, like a pendulum, between your image or memory of that experience and the current sensations in your body.

Now, think about something that happened in the last several weeks, when, again, you most felt like yourself or the person you'd like to be. Shift your awareness back and forth between the memory then and your current bodily experience. Stay with this experience for a few minutes without judging it, simply noticing what's bubbling up.

Repeat the same process, only this time go further back—to a month or so when you most felt like your authentic, integrity-driven, whole self. As you swing back and forth between your remembrance and the sensation, and from the sensation to the remembrance, allow the sensation to grow so you can feel it in your entire body.

Now, slowly start to open your eyes and locate your surroundings. Notice what your overall experience is *now*.

⟋ Pause and Appreciate ⟍

Grounding in Awareness is the first step to engaging your moral pain or soul wound and getting on the path of healing and wholeness. It's not easy to recount these kinds of painful experiences, even on paper and in the privacy of your own space. Take a moment to honor the important work you've done and the courage it took to Ground in Awareness.

Next up, Honor the Past.

*Sometimes the miracle is not
in the restoration of what was,
but in the courage to reconcile
yourself to what is, and flourish
because of it.*

PART 2

Honor the Past

There is no getting around the fact that moral pain and traumatic injury are genuine, irreducible, and crushing. So, why *honor the past*? Won't this only increase your distress?

Muscling the past into some old memory trunk and burying it deep within an internal emotional graveyard is simply selective amnesia—an unproductive and unsustainable escapist strategy that forces you to cut off from important aspects of who you are and from events or people that have shaped your life to this point. It's a recipe for an incoherent, disjointed life, filled with distraction, denial, and distortion—which is *no life at all.*

What's also unhealthy is wallowing in the past, or constantly reliving past traumas, offenses, or distressing experiences. In fact, it can be extremely destructive.

The key to engaging the past is fitting it with the right lens. When you Honor the Past, you're not saying the events that caused your moral pain are unimportant or just. Rather, you are affirming that *every* aspect of life—good, bad, happy, sad, joyful, or painful—has a key role to play in making you who you are today and who you'll be tomorrow. Moreover, you are affirming that in *every* life experience, including distressing ones, there is a *kernel of truth*—a message or meaning, an insight, that is inherently worthy and honorable to carry with you, and even inspire you going forward. In pain, there are *always* seeds of hope to plant.

The challenge of and opportunity for Honoring the Past lies not in vanquishing or forgetting your pain, nor condoning past wrongs or minimizing hurt. Rather, it's in finding that sacred kernel of truth and nourishing those seeds of hope as sources for growth, empowerment, and reconnecting with that deepest, most essential part of you.

CENTERING EXERCISE

TENSION RELEASE

Moral pain can greatly affect your tension level, especially the neck and shoulders, where all conscious thoughts collect.

1. Find somewhere comfortable to sit or lie down. It can be more effective to stretch out, but a comfy chair can work as well. Unfold your arms, uncross your legs (and if sitting, be sure to keep your feet flat on the floor), and begin to allow your attention to focus inward.

2. Close your eyes (if you feel comfortable) and bring your awareness to your head. Start by tensing the muscles in your face and scalp. Make a tight grimace; tighten your closed eyes and furrow your brow; clench your jaw; move your ears if you can.

3. Inhale slowly and evenly for a count of eight. Then exhale the same count, letting your face become completely relaxed as though you were sleeping. Notice any cracks, shifts, or releases that occur as a result. Repeat two or three times or until you feel those areas are at ease.

4. Next, move on to your neck and shoulders. Tense each area again, inhaling for eight, and exhaling the same while relaxing. Again, take notice of any inner sensations.

5. Continue to work your way down your body, stopping at each of the major muscle groups: your chest, abdomen and pelvis, arms and hands, and legs and feet.

6. When you're finished, open your eyes and bring them to a point in front of you. Take one final deep and steady inhale and exhale as you reorient to your surroundings.

✧ PROMPT 6 ✧

Mirror Test

This prompt has four parts. It can be done in one or more writing sessions.

PART 1: MIRROR TO THE PAST

Imagine you're holding a mirror to yourself before this violation happened. What do you see? Reflect on, then record, this image.

_____

_____

_____

_____

_____

_____

_____

_____

_____

Note how it feels to look at your past reflection. What emotions, sensations, and feelings bubble up? Note what messages they are sending.

_____

_____

_____

_____

_____

_____

_____

_____

_____

_____

_____

_____

_____

_____

PART 2: MIRROR ON NOW

Imagine holding up that same mirror to yourself today. Reflect on, then record, what you see.

_____

_____

_____

_____

_____

_____

_____

_____

_____

_____

_____

_____

_____

_____

PART 3: MIRROR ON YOUR EYES ONLY

Finally, focus your imagination on only your eyes. If they could speak then and now, what do they say about what they've seen?

_____

_____

_____

_____

_____

_____

_____

_____

_____

_____

_____

_____

_____

_____

_____

_____

PART 4: MIRROR OF CHANGE

What is the biggest difference you can detect between the images of then and now?

What is most meaningful about that change? Write down the messages that are being sent about how this moral injury or soul wound has changed you. Record what this says about your ability to heal and move forward.

_____

_____

_____

_____

_____

_____

_____

_____

_____

_____

_____

_____

_____

❧ Post-Writing Check-In ❧

Take a few moments to sit quietly without looking at what you wrote to transition to the present. Taking a few deep and quiet breaths can help. Mark how you're feeling in this moment on the scales below and jot down any thoughts that arise.

How distressed are you feeling in this moment?	How connected to others and life are you feeling in this moment?
(none) 0 1 2 3 4 5 6 7 8 9 10 (extremely)	(none) 0 1 2 3 4 5 6 7 8 9 10 (extremely)

❧ PROMPT 7 ❧

Web of Life

Imagine a web that holds important relationships in your life. For instance, family, friends, work, communities, or groups. Allow images of the most important ones to come forward. Reflect on, then record, what about those relationships was most important *before* your moral pain or soul wound. Drop into feelings and sensations and note what arises.

_____

_____

_____

_____

_____

_____

_____

_____

_____

_____

_____

_____

_____

Now, reflect on, then record, how your relationship with those people or groups has been affected by the experience. Again, drop into those feelings and sensations and note what messages they are sending.

_____

_____

_____

_____

_____

_____

_____

_____

_____

_____

What does this tell you about your ability to connect with others *now*?

_____

_____

ᥴᦾ Post-Writing Check-In ᥴᦾ

Take a few moments to sit quietly without looking at what you wrote to transition to the present. Taking a few deep and quiet breaths can help. Mark how you're feeling in this moment on the scales below and jot down any thoughts that arise.

How distressed are you feeling in this moment?	How connected to others and life are you feeling in this moment?
(none) 0 1 2 3 4 5 6 7 8 9 10 (extremely)	(none) 0 1 2 3 4 5 6 7 8 9 10 (extremely)

CONCLUDING EXERCISE

OPENING YOUR HEART

Find a comfortable place to sit. Bring your hands to your shoulders, elbows facing forward. Inhale as you expand wide across your chest. Open your elbows as far as they'll go and slowly lift your chin. Exhale as you pull your elbows into the front of your heart and tuck in your chin. Breathe deeply for a count of eight, focusing on your inhalation. Repeat until you feel something shift. (Don't worry if it doesn't happen right away. Keep going. It will.)

Now, consider what messages about yourself this violation has sent. Again, bring your hands to your shoulders and inhale, opening your chest and exhale, pulling in your elbows and chin. As you breathe deeply, notice any sensations wriggling about and what messages are coming through.

Next, consider all the work you've done so far in writing about Honor the Past: what emotions and feelings have been most activated? Repeat the technique above. Again, as you breathe deeply, notice any sensations and the messages that are accompanying them.

Write these messages down.

_____

_____

_____

_____

_____

Which negative "I" statement ("I'm powerless," "I'm inferior," "I'm damaged," "I don't deserve," etc.) best describes any messages about your experience of moral trauma or adversity? Note the emotions that accompany it.

_____

_____

_____

_____

Then trace that message's emotional lineage: can you recall other times in your life when you experienced the same message and feelings? How early does it go back? As before, breathe deeply and notice the sensations and messages coming through.

_____

_____

_____

_____

_____

_____

_____

_____

❧ Pause and Appreciate ❧

Honoring the Past is an emotionally arduous process. It asks a lot, but also gives a lot. Take a moment now to congratulate yourself on the important work you've done in Honoring the Past.

Next up, Transform the Present.

Hold the greatest thing you'll

never own...this moment.

PART 3

Transform the Present

Life is deeply complex—and quite simple. We're born. We live. We die. As Jean-Paul Sartre pointed out, "Everything has been figured out, except how to live." We alone are responsible for who we are and how we act. We may not always like the options at hand; we may feel like we've been given a raw deal, or that the deck is stacked against us, or that the system has failed or isn't made for us. And all those feelings may have elements of truth. And still, we must live—*now*. The only question is how?

Trust is the answer—and this starts with trust in ourselves.

Things happen. We can't pretend they haven't or won't. We can't always protect ourselves or others against them happening. And we can't "live in bad faith," becoming passive or checking out, when they do.

Transforming the Present comes down to facing fear. Fear is an innate self-preservation mechanism, but like all machines, sometimes our "self" goes awry. One of those wrenches in our system is rumination. Ruminating is the addictive repetition of a thought—usually a negative, fear-based one—without action or completion. We get trapped in our own heads, cycling through unpleasant or unreconciled experiences of the past or else what might (or might not) happen in the future. At its core, rumination is a heightened state of self-protection. The problem is that when we're in that state, we can't be open to learning new things.

How do we learn to trust life again after it threw us into a situation that violated the values, beliefs, and ideals we hold most dear, tearing at our soul? How do we come to embrace the truth that the same life that brings us pain also brings us joy? How do we affirm that hope, happiness, possibility, and peace can still be ours—and that we're *worthy* of it?

Being in the present moment is, perhaps paradoxically, the ultimate protection because fear does not exist there—there is only opportunity and choice.

CENTERING EXERCISE

FIND YOUR CENTER

The purpose of this exercise is to locate your physical center of gravity, which, during centering, is typically visualized as being two inches below your navel.

Sit now and get familiar with your center.

Pull your muscles in and out. Shift around to see how this center holds or stabilizes you. Remember what this feels like. Once you've found it, breathe deeply from your center and feel the sense of being firmly rooted in the ground.

Whenever you feel distressed or overwhelmed, or when it seems that your moral pain is seeping into the present and causing you to ruminate, bring attention to this center as a reminder that you have strength and self-command.

✑ PROMPT 8 ✑

Bittersweet

This prompt is a variation of the "Lemons Are Not Lemons" exercise developed by Wyatt R. Evans and colleagues (2020).

Imagine you're holding a fresh, picked lemon in your hands. Notice how the lemon *looks*: its vibrant yellow, oval shape, tiny dimples in its thick skin. Take time to turn the lemon over in your hands and really *see* it.

Now, imagine the way the lemon *feels*. Touch its texture—smooth or rough. Squeeze and press your fingers into the lemon and notice if it's firm or squishy. Notice how heavy or light it feels as you roll it around your palm.

Next, imagine your fingernails piercing the skin of the lemon. Notice how it *sounds* when it breaks opens. Slowly pull the lemon apart and notice what you hear as you tear it apart.

Imagine bringing one part of the lemon up to your face and inhaling deeply through your nose, paying attention to the *scent* of the lemon. Imagine its tangy aroma. As you smell the lemon's fragrant tartness, notice if your mouth begins to water.

Finally, bring that same part of the lemon to your mouth and take a big bite, *tasting* the fruit. Notice your body's reactions: maybe your lips pucker or smack; your jaw may clench; or you may scrunch up your face. As these things happen, continue to slowly chew the lemon and notice the taste.

Now, imagine swallowing the last of the bitter lemon. As you do, allow equally "bitter" words and phrases to form in your mind that you have used to describe yourself and/or others who may have violated or harmed you. Write them down.

Drop into the emotions and sensations that you feel bubbling up in your body. Maybe it's a heaviness or sharp pain, or the urge to get up and move away. Reflect on, then record, what this says about how your mind is holding you hostage to your bitter thoughts.

Just as you weren't literally holding a lemon because you thought about a lemon, you aren't literally broken, bad, evil, or helpless because your mind holds those thoughts.

⤳ Post-Writing Check-In ⤳

Take a few moments to sit quietly without looking at what you wrote to transition to the present. Taking a few deep and quiet breaths can help. Mark how you're feeling in this moment on the scales below and jot down any thoughts that arise.

How distressed are you feeling in this moment?	How connected to others and life are you feeling in this moment?
(none) 0 1 2 3 4 5 6 7 8 9 10 (extremely)	(none) 0 1 2 3 4 5 6 7 8 9 10 (extremely)

⤳ PROMPT 9 ⤳

Landscape of Life

Imagine you're a bird soaring over the landscape of your life—all the accidents, curiosities, oddities, synchronicities, troubles, joys, tragedies, and triumphs. What does it look like? A mountainous terrain, a rocky coast, a dense forest, or something else? As an image or images begin to form, start writing what you see in detail.

_____

_____

_____

_____

_____

_____

_____

_____

_____

_____

When you're done, choose five "marker moments" along that landscape that stand out—not necessarily because you judge them as either good or bad but rather because they are particularly meaningful and have some moral dimension or complexity.

1. _____

2. _____

3. _____

4. _____

5. _____

Now, imagine swooping down into each of those moments so that you're back on the ground as the events or experiences were unfolding at the time. Reflect on, then record, how your mind and heart were in conflict, pulling you in different directions between thinking and feeling. Drop into those sensations and note what you sense and what were the messages that you took away.

_____

_____

_____

_____

_____

Next, flap your wings and take back off into the sky. Looking down and back from today's vantage point, what more can you see in these experiences? Are there new kernels of truth? Perhaps a broader, more compassionate way of understanding the situation? Maybe there are some positive experiences or new connections that grew out of these events?

Drop into those sensations and record, then reflect on, what you sense and what messages you can take away from this moral pain or soul wound that helps you see it as one among many marker moments in your life.

⟋ Post-Writing Check-In ⟍

Take a few moments to sit quietly without looking at what you wrote to transition to the present. Taking a few deep and quiet breaths can help. Mark how you're feeling in this moment on the scales below and jot down any thoughts that arise.

How distressed are you feeling in this moment?	How connected to others and life are you feeling in this moment?
(none) 0 1 2 3 4 5 6 7 8 9 10 (extremely)	(none) 0 1 2 3 4 5 6 7 8 9 10 (extremely)

Use this space to reflect on the writing—how it felt, what was inspiring or challenging.

✎ PROMPT 10 ✎

Feel to Forgive, Reconcile to Restore

This prompt has several parts. It can be done in one or more writing sessions.

Often, moral harm or soul wounds cause us to become our own worst enemy. We become survivors, victims, or martyrs. We work against our own best interests. We stop showing up for life and taking responsibility for our life. We get trapped in our heads, dwelling on past grievances, personal histories, lost dreams, and abandoned hopes. We allow ourselves to get sucked into an existential vacuum, forgetting how to really live—and live *now*.

A key part of trusting ourselves again, or regaining our trust in others, is forgiveness. None of us is perfect, as much as we may wish it or aspire to it. And all of us have regrets. Sometimes, life throws us into impossible situations where no outcome is good and we or others must make impossible decisions under great duress. What matters is that you're treating yourself with *benevolent honesty*, that is, a kindness and gentleness so that you can reconcile difficult truths and find forgiveness.

Take a moment to explore the idea of forgiving yourself or someone else. Does it seem daunting, possible, or welcome?

Now, imagine your moral pain or soul wound is a massive bag of rocks strapped to your back or chest. Write about what it feels like to carry it throughout the day, to sleep and wake with it, to get close to others with it on. What's happening to your breath and your heart rate as you carry it? How is it affecting your energy level? What do you do or turn to when the burden becomes too heavy? Vices? Self-destructive behavior?

Next, imagine you're looking inside the bag at all the different-sized rocks and each one represents a grievance you're holding against yourself or others. Reflect on, then record, those grievances. As you do, notice what emotions, sensations, and feelings come up and note the messages they're sending.

Then, just for a moment, imagine yourself taking the heavy bag off your body and setting it down beside you. What's happening as you do? What is your heart doing? Your breath, muscles, energy? If it's hard to give yourself permission to take the bag off, just take a few deep breaths and imagine reaching out, touching the bag, then setting it down. Notice the lightness and freedom of no longer carrying the heavy burden. Breathe deeply into the relief for as long as you can. Then write about what it felt like to set aside the burden, even for a moment.

When you're ready, reflect on and record how you are affected by punishing yourself and/or others by continuing to carry this heavy burden.

_____

_____

_____

_____

_____

_____

_____

Also, consider how others are affected by you continuing to carry it. Has carrying it led to a correction in terms of living your values and improving your relationships, or has it made things worse?

_____

_____

_____

_____

_____

_____

What does it feel like when you don't forgive yourself and/or others and continue to carry this burden? What other important values are you sacrificing?

What bonds or connections do you miss out on by *not* forgiving yourself or someone else by carrying the weight?

Now, imagine yourself standing up and walking away from the heavy bag of grievances or broken promises. What does it feel like to no longer be burdened by its weight on your body and soul?

_____

_____

_____

_____

_____

_____

Reflect on and record how your life might change without the bag strapped to you.

_____

_____

_____

_____

_____

_____

How might it affect others you care for and your relationships with them if you were free of this burden?

∽ Post-Writing Check-In ∽

Take a few moments to sit quietly without looking at what you wrote to transition to the present. Taking a few deep and quiet breaths can help. Mark how you're feeling in this moment on the scales below and jot down any thoughts that arise.

How distressed are you feeling in this moment?	How connected to others and life are you feeling in this moment?
(none) 0 1 2 3 4 5 6 7 8 9 10 (extremely)	(none) 0 1 2 3 4 5 6 7 8 9 10 (extremely)

∾ PROMPT 11 ∾

Values Compass Reset

Many people who struggle with moral pain feel as though their moral compass is broken. The violation that resulted from their actions or others' actions leaves them feeling like captives in a strange new world where the familiar still looks the same, but somehow the way they feel about the familiar, and their relationship to it, is suddenly different. It's as if they've become alienated from their "normal" valued world—everyone and everything else is going about life as usual. But for them, "normal" is no more; it's broken, never to return.

Consider this: just because you *feel* moral pain doesn't mean that you or your moral compass is broken. To the contrary, that pain is a beacon signaling to your body and soul that your compass is still very much in working order. It's more likely that you have veered off course to escape the pain and now you're lost and stuck without an obvious marker for the path back to your life's journey.

This prompt will serve as a guide to get you back on the path of integrity and connection. Start by reading through the list of values. Go slowly, dropping into sensations as you read each one. Be sure to go through the entire list before writing.

✂ VALUES LIST ✂

Acceptance	Dignity	Initiative	Respect
Accountability	Diversity	Integrity	Responsibility
Achievement	Environment	Intuition	Safety
Adaptability	Equality	Joy	Security
Adventure	Excellence	Kindness	Self-awareness
Altruism	Fairness	Knowledge	Self-development
Ambition	Faith	Learning	Self-discipline
Authenticity	Family	Love	Self-expression
Balance	Forgiveness	Loyalty	Sexuality
Beauty	Freedom	Making a difference	Simplicity
Career	Friendship	Open-mindedness	Spirituality
Collaboration	Fun	Order	Success
Commitment	Generosity	Patience	Thrift
Community	Grace	Patriotism	Tradition
Compassion	Gratitude	Peace	Trust
Competence	Health	Perseverance	Truth
Confidence	Honesty	Pleasure	Uniqueness
Connection	Hope	Power	Wealth
Contribution	Humility	Reliability	Well-being
Courage	Humor	Resourcefulness	Wisdom
Creativity	Inclusion		
Curiosity	Independence		

Go through this list again and cross out any values that don't resonate with you.

Now, go through the values that remain and place a check mark next to all those that are of high importance to you now, even if you're not living them in the way that you would like.

Next, underline your top five values and rank them from 1 to 5. This may be challenging because each value may seem as important as the others, but try to rank them regardless.

1. _____

2. _____

3. _____

4. _____

5. _____

Now, imagine a time when you used those prized values to good end. Wander around the memory for a time, dropping into the feelings, emotions, and sensations as you do. Reflect on, and record, what it felt like to apply them in real life and what messages that sent you about yourself.

_____

_____

_____

_____

Finally, consider the values that were violated and led to your ongoing experience of moral pain. Circle as many as you like and note which ones overlap with your top five values. Take a moment to drop into the feelings, emotions, and sensations that arise and listen for messages about what that tells you about your moral compass. Reflect on and record what surfaces.

∽ Post-Writing Check-In ∽

Take a few moments to sit quietly without looking at what you wrote to transition to the present. Taking a few deep and quiet breaths can help. Mark how you're feeling in this moment on the scales below and jot down any thoughts that arise.

How distressed are you feeling in this moment?	How connected to others and life are you feeling in this moment?
(none) 0 1 2 3 4 5 6 7 8 9 10 (extremely)	(none) 0 1 2 3 4 5 6 7 8 9 10 (extremely)

CONCLUDING EXERCISE

VITAL MOMENTS

Many people struggling with moral pain ruminate. That is the addictive process of getting trapped in the mind, cycling through unpleasant or unreconciled experiences of the past or disconcerting thoughts about what might (or might not) happen in the future. Sometimes, the cycling becomes so all-consuming that what's happening in the here-and-now becomes fused with what happened then. This leads to harsh judgments and criticism about their or others' previous actions, as well as ominous projections about their fate: "My life is forever doomed," "Justice will never be served," "Fairness is an illusion," "Healing is not possible." With the present now sullied by these criticisms and projections, all the hours of the day feel bleak, hopeless, and without vitality.

One way to break this cycle of criticism is through kindness.

Imagine a time when you got caught up in that dizzying ruminating cycle. Take a minute to drop into the emotions, feelings, and sensations that bubble up. Then reflect on, and record, what specific messages the experience sent.

_____

_____

_____

_____

Now, imagine a time when someone was kind to you. Maybe that's a family member or friend, a teacher or mentor, or even a stranger. Remember and record everything you can about the experience—the words, gestures, touches, or actions the kind person used that soothed or helped you or made your life just a little better in the moment. As the memory becomes clear, describe what you see, hear, smell, or feel on your skin as if you were back there now. Put a name to the emotion, when you felt it, both then and now as you recall the experience.

If any negative feelings from the past or concerns for the present arise, imagine setting them in a bottle on a high shelf, then come back to the kind memory.

ᥦ Pause and Appreciate ᥦ

Transforming the Present takes courage. Like Grounding in Awareness and Honoring the Past, it asks a lot, but also it gives a lot. Take a moment now to congratulate yourself on the important work you've done in Transforming the Present.

Next up, Reimagine the Future.

We are often our own worst enemy,
but are always our best possibility.

PART 4

Reimagine the Future

None of us is born thinking about what the future holds and yet we are born with the ability to "pre-experience" it through our imagination. This future-minded superpower is called "prospection." It's a skill that human beings developed to a distinct degree; however, we aren't alone in having it: even dogs get excited at the appearance of a leash or a cat at the sound of a can opening.

One of the primary functions of prospection is that it influences how we act. Thinking about ourselves in the future helps us decide what to do "now." In this way, the stories we tell ourselves about the future can be as influential as the ones we tell about the past. They, too, can empower us or else confine us—it's our choice. When we take ownership of our stories, live by the "right" stories, and connect the stories from the past to the future, we gain a much desired "coherent sense of time" (DeMarco, 2024), as I call it, that our soul wound stole.

Our story of moral harm is a story within a story. In fact, it's a story within a series of stories that make up the story of our lives. To craft that larger story, we must first rewrite a new story for that painful experience.

Rewriting the Future is not about creating a make-believe tale that pretties up or glosses over the bad bits, nor is it about wish fulfillment gone wild. It's simply telling the experience from an expanded, coherent perspective that you've gained from this journal so far. It means mindfully putting words to a story that is *true for you* in a way that is benevolently honest and grounded in hope.

CENTERING EXERCISE

INTEGRAL ENERGY

This exercise is adapted from Aikido, meaning "the way of harmonizing energy." It is a Japanese form of martial art that leverages momentum and resistance to deflect rather than overpower one's opponent.

Start by finding somewhere comfortable to sit so that your feet are connected to the ground. Exhale a long, even breath, and as you do, visualize that breath weaving down into the earth as roots would a tree, grounding you. Next, inhale and imagine the breath cascading over you from above, like a cleansing waterfall. Feel it washing away any pent-up stress, any toxins floating around inside. Relax as you concentrate on your vertical core. Roll your shoulders back; stretch your neck up; allow your chest to widen. Feel integrity with this dignified posture.

Now, sense the space around you. Imagine a color or your soul (or inner light) radiating in waves from your body in all directions. See yourself at its center.

Feel the weight of your body resting into the earth beneath you—your arms, legs, feet, and jaw all supported. Then feel the lightness of your soul in the air above and around you. Notice what it feels like to be supported by all these life-sustaining elements.

Now, reflect on each of the Six Fundamental Human Desires from the earlier prompt: meaning, purpose, value, connection, resilience, and transcendence. Allow your mind to ask your soul and body what it would feel like to have more of each. Picture yourself doing something that brings on those feelings. Savor the experience.

❧ PROMPT 12 ❧

Three "S" Selves

Research on moral emotions shows that when people's morals or values are violated, often their beliefs about themselves or others become harsher and more rigid. This could be one reason why people with soul wounds have a particularly hard time with compassion. Compassion is often seen as weak or a "soft" emotion, or else something unwarranted, undeserved, indulgent, or inappropriate.

And yet, compassion is key to relieving moral pain and restoring right relationships.

Compassion is the recognition of our own or others' suffering with a desire to try to alleviate and prevent that suffering. This is different from empathy, which allows us to take the perspective of another person and to feel the emotions of another person, whether positive or negative. Compassion emerges when those empathetic thoughts and feelings include a commitment to help. It gives us the courage to *turn toward* suffering while giving us the strength to not only feel pain but also overcome it. Compassion allows us to be present to others and ourselves in times of need (Neff, 2009).

This prompt asks you to imagine three different aspects of yourself: (1) the *Scared, Critical Self*; (2) the *Sensitive, Criticized Self* (the part of you that knows you are scared and being criticized and responds emotionally); and (3) the *Sacred, Benevolent Self* (a compassionate observer).

#1: SCARED, CRITICAL SELF

To begin, imagine three chairs side by side, each with a sign that displays these different aspects of self. Watch yourself moving toward and sitting in the one marked "Scared, Critical Self." Notice what the chair feels like beneath your weight and what sensations or emotions bubble up. Take a moment to drop into your moral pain, gently allowing the experience to form in your mind. Don't get stuck in the memory itself. Just rest in the reflection for a few moments, again dropping into emotions and sensations. Listen for fears and criticisms from this self—but don't push them away, even if it's hard. (It can also be helpful to record them.)

Now, go deep and listen hard, and speak aloud what this Scared, Critical Self is demanding that you know. For instance, "I am unlovable and unredeemable because of what I did;" "People will always betray me; the world is bad, and no one can be trusted;" or "God is punishing me because I'm a horrible person." As this self speaks to you, notice the tone of its voice, its facial expressions, and its body language. Also, pay attention to what emotions and sensations are bubbling up. (Use the distress tolerance techniques if you feel distressed or overwhelmed.)

Next, reflect on, and record, what it was like to sit in the Scared, Critical Self chair. What surprised or concerned you? What was it like to both hear and talk to yourself in this way? What messages did the experience send you?

#2: SENSITIVE, CRITICIZED SELF

Now, imagine yourself getting up and moving toward the chair marked "Sensitive, Criticized Self." Notice what the chair feels like beneath your weight and what sensations or emotions bubble up. Imagine you are hearing the fearful and critical thoughts just expressed by the Sensitive, Criticized Self; they are speaking with the same tone, expressions, and body language as before. Feel yourself embedded in that fear and receiving the criticism, then say aloud—directly to that Scared, Critical Self—what that experience makes you feel and think. For instance, "I feel worthless when you say that;" "That makes me shut down and pull away from everyone I love;" "I feel like I'm damned for all time." Again, as this self speaks to you, notice the tone of its voice, its facial expressions, and its body language. Also, pay attention to what emotions and sensations are bubbling up. (Use the distress tolerance techniques if you feel distressed or overwhelmed.)

Reflect on, and record, what it was like to sit in the Sensitive, Criticized Self's chair. What surprised or concerned you? What was it like to both hear and talk to yourself in this way? What messages did the experience send you?

#3: SACRED, BENEVOLENT SELF

Finally, imagine yourself getting up and moving toward the chair marked "Sacred, Benevolent Self"—the self who feels your suffering, is present to it, and has a desire to alleviate it. It can be helpful to imagine being someone you know who is trusted and holds deep wisdom, caring concern, and kindness, but make sure a part of you is still sitting in the chair just then. Notice what the chair feels like beneath your weight and what sensations or emotions bubble up. Anchor yourself firmly in the present. Notice how it feels to be in your benevolent and compassionate body. For instance, relaxed, relieved, at ease. Hold onto that feeling for a few moments.

Now, imagine that you can see the Scared, Critical Self and the Sensitive, Critical Self in front of you. Allow yourself to speak to each as the Sacred, Benevolent Self—with compassion and kindness. (You may want to speak these responses aloud before writing them down.)

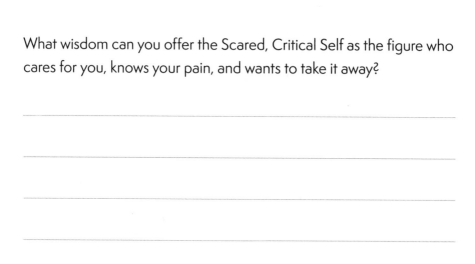

What wisdom can you offer the Scared, Critical Self as the figure who cares for you, knows your pain, and wants to take it away?

What compassionate insight can you offer to help the Scared, Critical Self see this experience in a broader and loving way?

In this moment, what kind words or gestures can you offer the Scared, Critical Self?

Next, allow the Sacred, Benevolent Self to respond to the Sensitive, Critical Self in the same way as above.

What wisdom can you offer the Sensitive, Critical Self as the figure who cares for you, knows your pain, and wants to take it away?

_____

_____

_____

_____

_____

What compassionate insight can you offer to help the Sensitive, Critical Self see this experience in a broader and loving way?

_____

_____

_____

_____

In this moment, what kind words or gestures can you offer the Sensitive, Critical Self?

Reflect on, and record, what it was like to sit in the Sacred, Benevolent Self chair. What surprised or concerned you? What was it like to both hear and talk to yourself in this way? What messages did the experience send you?

࿐ Post-Writing Check-In ࿐

Take a few moments to sit quietly without looking at what you wrote to transition to the present. Taking a few deep and quiet breaths can help. Mark how you're feeling in this moment on the scales below and jot down any thoughts that arise.

How distressed are you feeling in this moment?	How connected to others and life are you feeling in this moment?
(none) 0 1 2 3 4 5 6 7 8 9 10 (extremely)	(none) 0 1 2 3 4 5 6 7 8 9 10 (extremely)

❧ PROMPT 13 ☙

Words Made Real

The ancient Greek philosopher Plato told an allegory (or story) about an underground cave, where people are chained so deep that no sunlight reaches them. And if any of them were to be liberated and turned to look toward the light, they would suffer great distress and pain and be unable to see the realities of life.

Moral pain is like that cave: it holds people in a prison of darkness that warps their reality, disconnects them from others, and distances them from the light of life. But like Plato's cave, it's not that the light is bad; rather, it's that people are not used to seeing it.

Anyone who has become used to being in dark conditions will find it physically painful to adjust to the bright light of day, often squinting or covering their eyes to get back to the pain-free darkness. For some people without light for prolonged periods, that adjustment process may take time and can be helped along by wearing sunglasses.

When it comes to moral pain or soul wounds, four words serve as sunglasses to help you transition from the all-consuming darkness to the life-giving light. Those words are "acceptance," "compassion," "benevolence," and "courage." In these prompts, you will have the opportunity to explore each one, but for now, let's start orienting around each.

Imagine the word *acceptance* is a character that can speak. What kind of voice does it have? Ask Acceptance, "Who are you?" "Why are you important in my life?" Reflect on, then record, what it's like to hear Acceptance speak to you. Notice how the words make you feel. If at any time you start to feel distressed or overwhelmed, take a few deep breaths, and say to yourself, "I'm doing well. Just try to stay with the feeling a bit more." Consider what messages those sensations are carrying about your experience of moral pain or a soul wound.

_____

_____

_____

_____

_____

_____

_____

_____

_____

_____

Next, imagine the word *compassion* is a character that can speak. What kind of voice does it have? Ask Compassion, "Who are you?" "Why are you important in my life?" Reflect on, then record, what it's like to hear Compassion speak to you. Notice how the words make you feel. Consider what messages those sensations are carrying about your experience of moral injury or a soul wound.

Do the same exercise for the words *benevolence* (or *kindness*) and *courage*. When you're finished, pause for a moment to consider how, taken together, these "light-filled" words make you feel. It's okay if you still feel some "dark;" the point here is to get curious about how these words are living inside you and affecting your experience of moral pain.

❧ Post-Writing Check-In ❧

Take a few moments to sit quietly without looking at what you wrote to transition to the present. Taking a few deep and quiet breaths can help. Mark how you're feeling in this moment on the scales below and jot down any thoughts that arise.

How distressed are you feeling in this moment?	How connected to others and life are you feeling in this moment?
(none) 0 1 2 3 4 5 6 7 8 9 10 (extremely)	(none) 0 1 2 3 4 5 6 7 8 9 10 (extremely)

Use this space to reflect on the writing—how it felt, what was inspiring or challenging.

_____

_____

_____

_____

_____

_____

_____

_____

_____

❧ PROMPT 14 ❧

Revisioning Relationships

Moral values and the identities that sustain our relationships are the most important aspects of our lives; they constitute what is most sacred in us. Our sense that we are worth something and beloved by others lies at the heart of our relationships with them and the world. The violation of that worth—whether by our own actions or the actions of others—is an act of desecration and a fracture of trust. In this way, moral injury and moral distress are, at their core, relational. Healing hearts and repairing souls require a holistic process of reconnection to self-worth and life-sustaining relationships.

When we treat ourselves as sacred and with benevolence, or kindness, as we did in the preceding prompts, then we can free ourselves from the ruminating cycle of punishment that causes us to withdraw or engage in self- or other-loathing and myriad self-destructive behaviors. It also opens us up to re-envisioning important relationships, particularly those harmed by the violation.

Imagine a time before the experience that caused your soul wound, when you let yourself down (or others let you down) by acting or failing to act in a way that wasn't in line with your core values. Notice how you treated yourself (or them), particularly how you were kinder—maybe less critical or judgmental, or that you (or they) still had worth, or that you (or they) still deserved to be a part of the community of life. Drop into the feelings, emotions, and sensations that bubble up. Reflect on, then record, what that experience was like and what messages you discovered.

Now, imagine the ways you have punished yourself or others for this moral injury or soul wound. Drop into the feelings, emotions, and sensations that bubble up. Reflect on, then record, how your two responses differed. What messages does this send about your ability to forgive, reconcile, and act with compassion?

_____

_____

_____

_____

_____

_____

_____

_____

_____

_____

_____

_____

Next, imagine your Sacred, Benevolent Self (from the previous prompt) is sitting across from you, asking what you would need to treat yourself that way again. Drop into the feelings, emotions, and sensations that bubble up as you consider your response. Reflect on, and record, what they are telling you. Consider also what might get in the way.

Finally, imagine you are now your Sacred, Benevolent Self (from the previous prompt). Again, drop into the feelings, emotions, and sensations that bubble up as you consider your response to the following questions:

What has helped you to survive your (or others') mistakes or missteps? What supports you in forgiving yourself (or others), having compassion with yourself (and others), and accepting yourself (or others)?

What works against you?

What resistance do you have now for forgiving yourself (or others)?

Is there anything you need to do before you can forgive yourself (or others)? Do you need to apologize, make amends, or offer reparations?

How have you learned from your (or others') mistakes or missteps?

What is the growth opportunity or "kernel of truth"?

What promise(s) can you make to yourself now that will serve your greater good?

❧ Post-Writing Check-In ❧

Take a few moments to sit quietly without looking at what you wrote to transition to the present. Taking a few deep and quiet breaths can help. Mark how you're feeling in this moment on the scales below and jot down any thoughts that arise.

How distressed are you feeling in this moment?	How connected to others and life are you feeling in this moment?
(none) 0 1 2 3 4 5 6 7 8 9 10 (extremely)	(none) 0 1 2 3 4 5 6 7 8 9 10 (extremely)

∽ PROMPT 15 ∽

Positive Intention

Positive intention is the idea that people are autonomous beings with free will and make choices because an action will somehow be beneficial to them, either in whole or in part.

With moral injury, people act—often under duress—in situations where the stakes are high and no outcome is good, knowing that they must choose a direction even though harm will come. It may seem paradoxical to think there could be positive intention in such damnable situations, but that would be shortsighted. Take, for instance, a doctor during the first phase of the COVID-19 pandemic who had to choose which patients were put on ventilators and which were, in all practicality, left to die. The positive intention there is that they were dutifully fulfilling their Hippocratic oath, even though the circumstances required they also break it. Or a worker who falsifies documents for fear of losing their job so that they could provide financial support for their sick child. The positive intention in this case is that they are trying to live up to their responsibilities as a parent *and* desperately trying to keep their child alive.

In finding positive intention, it's not that you are saying the violation was okay or are making excuses for the harm. Rather, it's about opening yourself up to new ways of thinking about the values underlying the harmful action, and then considering how those insights could be used differently for good going forward.

While it can be difficult to find positive intention in actions that may have been harmful or misguided, if you try to identify some positive intention and link it to your values, especially those you have in common, then it becomes easier to engage with people (or yourself) in a more compassionate way.

This prompt starts with finding a comfortable place to sit, making sure your feet are flat on the ground. Close your eyes, if you feel comfortable, and bring awareness to your soul wound. Take a few moments to gently drop into the moral pain and imagine the values that it violated and how that feels.

Next, imagine a glowing light, showering all that pain. Hold onto that image for a few moments, breathing slowly through each one.

Now, imagine your Sacred, Benevolent Self (the self who is kind and compassionate) is sitting across from you. It wants you to know that there may have been other values at play in this morally painful experience. Allow this self to tell you what those values were and why they were important. Drop into the sensations, feelings, and emotions that bubble up as you listen.

Reflect on, and record, what it was like to hear the Sacred, Benevolent Self share this positive intention.

What surprised or concerned you?

_____

_____

_____

_____

What messages did the experience send?

_____

_____

_____

What wisdom about this soul wound can you take away?

Let's take one step further and use positive intention to see how *all* the values that have influenced this moral injury or soul wound can open new doors and expand your horizon.

Reflect on, and record, the following sentences, filling in your responses:

> *I may have lost ... [fill in with something that was meaningful], but I have found ... [fill in with something that has new meaning]. And its gift is that ... [fill in with how this can be used in the future].*

Here is an example:

> *I may have lost the belief that I can control everything in life if I just try hard enough or do the right thing, but I have found that when I embrace the unknown, I feel more unencumbered and freer to try new things. And its gift is that I will be more confident about trusting myself and others in the future.*

Write your response.

⤸ Post-Writing Check-In ⤹

Take a few moments to sit quietly without looking at what you wrote to transition to the present. Taking a few deep and quiet breaths can help. Mark how you're feeling in this moment on the scales below and jot down any thoughts that arise.

How distressed are you feeling in this moment?	How connected to others and life are you feeling in this moment?
(none) 0 1 2 3 4 5 6 7 8 9 10 (extremely)	(none) 0 1 2 3 4 5 6 7 8 9 10 (extremely)

CONCLUDING EXERCISE

GENTLE HEART

This prompt is a variation of the Self-Holding exercise developed by Peter Levine (2010).

One of the most common refrains from people struggling with moral injury or moral distress is the sense of feeling divided—within themselves and from others and the world. This "aloneness" is the body and mind's way of trying to protect you from being hurt again or from hurting others. The problem is that isolation can be unbearable for the soul because ultimately, the soul wants to connect.

In this way, moral wounds are social wounds. They cut deep and separate us from our common humanity—that is, the awareness that all human beings are imperfect and limited. Bad things really do happen to good people, and sometimes for no good reason; physical pain (like illness, injury, exhaustion, old age, and eventually death) and emotional suffering (like fear, frustration, disappointment, and despair) are inescapable parts of life; and knowledge, as reliable as it can be, is sometimes flawed, so what we and others think we know, we sometimes don't. In other words, *all* humans suffer at some point in life. More to the point, most, if not all, humans have been on both sides of that suffering—both as the wounded and the wounder. Reconnecting with our common humanity through compassion will help you to feel less alone and have more connection with important others who care for you. It can also help you to reconcile wrongs done to you.

Start by finding a comfortable place to sit or lie down. If sitting, make sure your feet are flat on the floor. Close your eyes, if you feel comfortable, and bring awareness to your moral pain. Take a few moments to gently drop into that pain and imagine how it's pulled you away from others, life, and/or your Sacred Self.

Next, take a deep and gentle breath. As you exhale, place your right hand over your heart and your left hand on top of the right (If this feels silly, still do it—it helps). Go slow, breathing in and out, and notice what's going on:

- Notice the feelings and sensations of your hands resting on your heart and on one another. For example, maybe it's relaxing, comforting, energizing, or tingling. Pause for a moment to just be with these feelings and observe. (Sometimes, there are no words for what you sense. It's okay. Just be with the sensations as they shift and change for a while, even if you can't describe them.)

- Now feel inside your heart. What sensations are in there? Maybe a little tension or relaxation? You may even sense some emotions or colors or shapes or qualities, like slow wave motion or jagged textures or orange or red. Pause again to just be with these feelings and observe.

- Notice the warmth flowing from your hands into your chest. Notice soft pressure, pulsing, beating. Pause and observe. Let whatever sensations come.

- Notice any soothing sensations, peacefulness, benevolence, or a sense of connection and loving-kindness. Pause again to be with these feelings and observe.

- Now, you're going to shift positions. While still holding your right hand, slowly move your left hand to your right shoulder so that you are essentially giving yourself a hug. Breathe slowly and deeply into this posture, gently squeezing the hand on your shoulder. As you inhale, imagine a sense of compassion—visualize an image, hear a song or voice, imagine a touch. As you exhale, conjure the feeling of connection.

- Next, imagine moments of kindness in your life—when others have been kind to you and when you have been kind to others. Let those feelings course through your body, savoring each one.

- Finally, imagine a moment of feeling loved and cherished by someone. Pause and observe how that felt. Then remember a moment of you loving and cherishing someone, even a beloved pet. Allow the feeling of love to flow through your body. Then, pause and let yourself feel your own goodness.

Continue noticing the sensations in the space between your hands and heart and shoulder. Notice if they're shifting, for instance, softening, easing, or warming. Stay here for however long you'd like. There's no need to rush and no limit to the amount of benevolence and compassion you can send and receive.

When you're ready, reflect on, then record, what the experience was like of allowing yourself to receive these gifts. What messages about your ability to offer compassion to yourself and/or others emerged?

_____

_____

_____

_____

_____

_____

✑ Pause and Appreciate ✑

Reimagining the Future takes confidence. Like Grounding in Awareness, Honoring the Past, and Transforming the Present, it asks a lot, but also gives a lot. Take a moment now to congratulate yourself on the important work you've done in Reimagine the Future.

Next up, Soul Remaking.

*There is a light within each of us
that, when allowed to shine, will
illuminate the world.*

PART 5

Soul Remaking

The writing prompts throughout this book have focused on engaging your imagination, particularly your moral imagination, and sensory experience in a way that allows you to become more present to your moral pain not by denying it but rather by allowing that pain to be felt and better understood.

The following writing prompts are focused on what I call *Soul Remaking*, reimagining the circumstances that caused your moral injury or moral distress as a type of "calling" through which new purpose in life can be found. Soul Remaking allows your soul wound to be attended to not as an illness needing a cure, or a problem to solve, but as an artist or poet seeking to imbue life with new meaning.

If this sounds paradoxical, that's because it is—or at least it may appear to be given the painful and transgressive nature of the experience. But really, what this reimagining, shift-in-perspective does is allow you to respond to the worst experiences of your life with the best of yourself—to not be wholly and eternally defined by the violation. Instead, you can connect these painful experiences to your life's purpose: who will you become *now—because of* this experience. That life-affirming choice resides deep within you. By seizing that choice as an imperative that must be lived, the taint of the transgressive act is transformed, and in so doing, opens you up to rediscovering the trust, confidence, and connection that was lost because of your moral violation— reclaiming a sense of soulfulness.

CENTERING EXERCISE

ACCORDION

This technique is adapted from qigong, a centuries-old mind-body-spirit practice that balances our essential energy or vital life force (chi) by integrating posture, movement, and breathing. By using your hands like the bellow of an accordion or a bicycle pump, you can feel the flow of the force.

Start by closing your eyes halfway. Empty your mind and let your attention fall to your palms. Allow your breath to become slow, easy, without force, as though you are in the very lightest trance.

Next, bring your hands together, palms touching and fingers pointing upward. Slowly move your hands, keeping your palms aligned. When they are about twelve inches apart (or the width of your shoulders), slowly bring them together, using the least amount of effort possible. You will be compressing the air between them like an accordion. Feel a warm or tingling sensation in the middle of your palms.

Continue moving your hands slowly back and forth, varying the range and the direction of the bellows—horizontally, vertically, and diagonally.

✐ PROMPT 16 ✐

Symptom Symbols

Moral pain doesn't feel particularly good, which is one reason why so many people try to avoid it, often through alcohol or substance abuse, risky behavior, and other self-harming actions. The pain is also a reminder of the violation of your cherished values and can easily become fused with negative feelings and rigid and harsh beliefs.

And yet, as mentioned, the pain you feel—symptoms, such as shame, guilt, disgust, despair, disillusionment, emptiness, and isolation—is not a mark of your soul in tatters and beyond repair but rather just another expression of its voice calling out to be heard.

Imagine each of your symptoms are characters on a stage, and you're in the front row, looking up. Let each symptom come forward, announce itself, and tell you what its purpose in your life has been to this point. Hear its voice; watch the way it moves as it speaks, listen as it says to you, "*This* is what I need to you to know..."

Drop into the feelings, emotions, and sensations and notice what bubbles up.

What is it like to hear this ultimate message from each of your symptoms?

Focus on one symptom that you feel has been the most dominant in your life. Can you identify the way the symptom was trying to protect you? Describe it.

_____

_____

_____

_____

_____

_____

_____

Imagine that you are backstage, talking to that symptom. What now do _you_ need it to know? How has its performance in your life affected you?

_____

_____

_____

_____

Imagine what you can thank it for and let it know that its protection is no longer needed.

❧ Post-Writing Check-In ❧

Take a few moments to sit quietly without looking at what you wrote to transition to the present. Taking a few deep and quiet breaths can help. Mark how you're feeling in this moment on the scales below and jot down any thoughts that arise.

How distressed are you feeling in this moment?	How connected to others and life are you feeling in this moment?
(none) 0 1 2 3 4 5 6 7 8 9 10 (extremely)	(none) 0 1 2 3 4 5 6 7 8 9 10 (extremely)

∽ PROMPT 17 ∾

Accepting Risk

The Chinese philosopher Lao Tzu once said, "If you do not change direction, you may end up where you're heading." Unfortunately, change is not something that comes easy for most people; in fact, many of us seem to naturally want to fight against it. Of course, there's a simple reason: change casts us, like an abandoned stone, from our comfort zones into a vast sea of the unknown. And what we don't know, we can't control. And what we can't control, we often fear.

"What if I try and I fail?" "What if I trust and I'm let down or betrayed...again?" "What if it, or something like it, happens again.?" These fear-driven questions that often arise in the wake of moral pain are at the root of "controlled avoidance," the tendency to try to control or circumvent the consequences— like pain, shame, guilt, and so on—of your moral violation. These attempts are not only futile but also have high costs, particularly when it comes to your relationships and quality of life. Controlled avoidance robs you of the possibility and opportunity of healing from your moral injury or soul wound.

Changing direction requires taking healthy risks by engaging your moral imagination to step into the unknown, where peace, wholeness, and connection beckon. While you are neither guaranteed nor in control of the outcome, you can take command of yourself and "struggle well" in the uncertainty by being mindful of your feelings, thoughts, and values-based actions. In this way, in any moment, no matter how difficult or painful, you can make an intentional choice to follow your moral compass and live your values.

Imagine a fear-driven question, like the examples I've shared, that is on constant replay in your mind. Maybe this is about how you see yourself after this moral injury or soul wound; maybe it's how you see others. Maybe it has something to do with an important relationship that is strained or conflicted. What emotions, feelings, or sensations bubble up as the image appears?

_____

_____

_____

_____

Now, imagine you are standing on the edge of a tall cliff, and across the dark ravine below there is an inviting landscape with people you love and admire. Drop into the feelings and flickers deep inside and allow one's hope, connection, and peace to come to the surface. Hold onto them for a few moments, then imagine: what values you could employ to make the leap to the other side? Write down those values.

_____

_____

_____

_____

_____

_____

Imagine yourself holding onto those values or tucking them into a backpack as you step back and take a running leap, flying through the air, and landing safely on the inviting ground. Drop into these feelings, emotions, and sensations, and reflect, then record, what messages they're sending about what you need to take a healthy risk and change direction.

⤳ Post-Writing Check-In ⤳

Take a few moments to sit quietly without looking at what you wrote to transition to the present. Taking a few deep and quiet breaths can help. Mark how you're feeling in this moment on the scales below and jot down any thoughts that arise.

How distressed are you feeling in this moment?	How connected to others and life are you feeling in this moment?
(none) 0 1 2 3 4 5 6 7 8 9 10 (extremely)	(none) 0 1 2 3 4 5 6 7 8 9 10 (extremely)

✑ PROMPT 18 ✑

Your Calling, Your Purpose

Now that you've gotten the fullness of how this moral injury or soul wound has impacted your life—both in what was lost and what was found—it's time to reimagine the main message of your experience with, or story of, moral injury or soul wound—because every good story has one.

It's often thought that this main message is the moral of your story, but that's not the case. Your main message should be a statement on the human condition that your morally painful experience embodies. For instance,

> *We all have a tear in our lives, a hole in the center of us, an incompleteness that makes us vulnerable to attacks on our soul, but our soul can never be broken. Rather, it can only be lost sight of. Soul is always there to support us, to breathe life into us, no matter what happens; we just need to hold onto it.*

So, imagine now: what is the main message of *your* story with moral injury or a soul wound? Make room for images, symbols, and metaphors to help shape that message. Reflect on, then record this message, allowing yourself to drop into the feelings, emotions, and sensations that bubble up.

Now, imagine what this message is telling you about "your calling"—your purpose, a life-affirming imperative that now must be lived by you. Describe it as fully as you can.

∽ Post-Writing Check-In ∽

Take a few moments to sit quietly without looking at what you wrote to transition to the present. Taking a few deep and quiet breaths can help. Mark how you're feeling in this moment on the scales below and jot down any thoughts that arise.

How distressed are you feeling in this moment?	How connected to others and life are you feeling in this moment?
(none) 0 1 2 3 4 5 6 7 8 9 10 (extremely)	(none) 0 1 2 3 4 5 6 7 8 9 10 (extremely)

⌒ PROMPT 19 ⌒

Healing Haiku

A traditional Japanese haiku is a three-line poem with seventeen syllables, written in a 5/7/5-syllable count. Haiku focuses on a brief moment in time; uses provocative, colorful images, often from nature, that can be read in one breath—a sense of sudden enlightenment; and emphasizes simplicity, intensity, and directness of expression. For instance, this classic haiku by Kobayashi Issa written in the eighteenth century:

> *Everything I touch*
>
> *with tenderness, alas,*
>
> *pricks like a bramble.*

Or this classic by Masaoka Shiki:

> *A mountain village*
>
> *under the piled-up snow*
>
> *the sound of water.*

Haikus connect things that are often seen as separate. Writing haikus can help you plunge into the depths of your sacred, soulful self, or inner sanctum, and connect that self or sanctum with the outside world.

Imagine a provoking image from the past situation that caused your moral injury or soul wound. Allow this image to turn Technicolor in your mind, then drop into the sensations and feelings that it brings up. Reflect on, then record, one line with five syllables that is inspired by that image.

Now, imagine a provoking image that captures how you feel now, having engaged and written about your moral injury or soul wound. Again, allow this image to turn Technicolor in your mind and drop into the sensations and feelings that it brings up. Reflect on, then record, one line with seven syllables that is inspired by that image.

Finally, imagine a provoking image that captures how these past and present images are connected and expressed in the world. Once more, allow this image to turn Technicolor in your mind and drop into the sensations and feelings that it brings up. Reflect on, then record, one last line with five syllables that is inspired by that image.

When you're done, read through your healing haiku, then reflect on, then record what this inspires deep within you about how you are healing from moral injury or a soul wound.

∼ Post-Writing Check-In ∼

Take a few moments to sit quietly without looking at what you wrote to transition to the present. Taking a few deep and quiet breaths can help. Mark how you're feeling in this moment on the scales below and jot down any thoughts that arise.

How distressed are you feeling in this moment?	How connected to others and life are you feeling in this moment?
(none) 0 1 2 3 4 5 6 7 8 9 10 (extremely)	(none) 0 1 2 3 4 5 6 7 8 9 10 (extremely)

❧ Pause and Appreciate ❧

Soul Remaking takes, well, soul. Like the earlier sections, it asks a lot, but also gives a lot. Take a moment now to congratulate yourself on the important work you've done in Soul Remaking.

Last up, Forward into New Life!

We cannot recreate our lives
going backward.
We can only reclaim our life
moving forward.

PART 6

Forward into New Life

Conscience is the indestructible core of our personal identity and our sense of agency in the world, and when it passes judgment against us, it generates inner conflict—that is, moral injury or a soul wound. Its emotions are so powerful and destructive that facing them is akin to sitting in a consuming fire that threatens our very existence. Only when we can feel, acknowledge, reflect on, and share our soul pain by sitting in that fire can we burn clean and rise from the ashes to find new meaning and purpose in life, like the fabled ancient phoenix that emerges from its own ashes renewed. With moral injury or moral distress, renewal means integrating our painful experiences as sources of wisdom and guidance that enable us to both reclaim and maintain our relationship with ourselves, families, friends, and communities—with all of life, really.

That process of integration is ongoing; it requires awareness and intention at each step as you move forward into new life. Because your moral pain is linked to the morally injurious or distressing experience, and because your soul is linked to your purpose or calling, living that purpose or fulfilling that calling with committed action means that your moral pain may, again, make itself known. Being willing to hold that pain in the service of something good—your purpose and values—at the same time moving forward with new life is essential for fully integrating your experience and finding renewal.

The final two prompts will help you to simultaneously hold the remnants of moral pain and seeds of hope and to reconnect fully as you move forward into new life.

149

CENTERING EXERCISE

BLENDING

This practice also comes from qigong. It helps you become aware of energy resonating through you and blend it into an even flow.

Begin by standing with your feet shoulder's width apart and your knees slightly bent. Allow your arms and hands to hang at your sides. Shift your weight slightly onto the balls of your feet. Bring your awareness to the front side of your body. Concentrate on the channels that pass along the front of your legs and torso, the top of your hands and arms, and your face. After a minute or so, shift your weight onto your heels. Become aware of the back of your body—the back of your head and your arms, spine, and legs. (With practice, you can increase the time that you hold these postures.)

You can also repeat this practice for the left and right sides of your body. In each instance, you may want to become aware of each section of the body. For example, the side of your head, the side of your arm and torso, your outer hip, the side of your leg and ankle, and the length of your foot. This makes the exercise a meditation.

If you're feeling adventurous, now try repeating the first three steps, but keep the motion fluid, visually undetectable. Continue shifting your weight forward and backward, feeling your energy flowing along the front and back of your body. Then, try to feel it flowing along your back and front simultaneously.

∽ PROMPT 20 ∽

Sensing Soul

Eugene Gendlin, an American philosopher, thought that the human body is the primary way individuals create meaning out of an experience; he referred to it as "felt sense" (1978). Felt sense is essentially a combination of emotion, awareness, intuitiveness, and embodiment that is hard to put into words, but gives us the sense of "something." This something contains essential information about understanding psychic or emotional issues a person is facing.

Many people with moral injury or soul wounds feel as though they have lost their sense of soul. Through the writing prompts in this journal, perhaps you've sensed a soulful flicker. Now, it's time to engage soul more directly.

Imagine letting yourself go...and letting yourself be. Close your eyes slowly and start to ease your body. Gently breathe in. And gently breathe out. Allow all the tension from the process to slowly fall away. Feel the muscles in your body begin to give way. Allow your feet to get loose and heavy. Let your ankles drop toward the floor. Feel your calves and thighs getting limp, your hips and pelvis drawing downward. Let your stomach and back relax from all the stress they have been carrying. Feel your arms growing longer. Feel your shoulders fall. Allow your jaw and eyes to droop.

Next, focus on your breath. Breathe in through your nose and out through your mouth. Move the air slowly, evenly, deeply. Feel yourself aligning with the natural flow of life. As you do, feel a sense of soul begin to reveal itself. Feel yourself calmer, more connected, and more at ease.

Now, turn your attention deeper within, to the place that only you can go—to the center of your being, the home of your soul. That sacred space, your inner sanctum, beyond all your thoughts and skills. Beyond all your worries and concerns. Beyond all the drama and distraction, all the sadness and suffering that has held you back and cloaked your life in a tattered veil. Feel the warmth, the light, the energy of authenticity pulsating in time with your heart.

You are not your fears. You are not the characters others may want you to play—or the characters that you *think* you should play or now need to play. You are a Sacred Self. A connected being.

Journey now to this sacred center. Allow yourself to fall into it freely. As you breathe in and out, imagine the words, "I am." As you breathe out, imagine the words, "I can." In this inner sanctum, feel the warmth, the light, the energy of your soul pulsing in time with your heart. Repeat the words, "Healing comes from soulful seeing and being."

Now, imagine yourself as a child. What dreams did you have? What were your hopes for your future self? As you breathe in, imagine the words, "I am." As you breathe out, imagine the words, "I can."

Now, imagine your future self. Sit with this image for a few moments. As you become more and more present to it, feel its light and peace. Allow yourself to step into this image and become fully this person. Become who you have always been. Become who you are. Become who you can and will always be. Just for this moment, just be. This is your authentic, sacred, and soulful self.

When you're ready, pay attention to your breathing once again. And begin to come back into your body, holding onto the image of your authentic, sacred, and soulful self. As you feel your muscles reawakening, and your body replenishing itself with energy, repeat the words, "Help me to feel as I am, think as I can, and live as I ought." Or if you prefer, "I promise to feel as I am, think as I can, and live as I ought."

Open your eyes slowly, feeling centered, connected, and renewed. Sit quietly for a moment, as you reacclimate to your surroundings.

Now, reflect on, and record, what it was like to sense your soul. It doesn't matter how long the experience was—just a few flickers or a flood—drop into the feelings, emotions, and sensations that bubble up. Consider what messages they are sending about your ability to reconnect your soul. What does your soul want to say, to do, to be, to express, to relate to, and to connect with?

∾ Post-Writing Check-In ∾

Take a few moments to sit quietly without looking at what you wrote to transition to the present. Taking a few deep and quiet breaths can help. Mark how you're feeling in this moment on the scales below and jot down any thoughts that arise.

How distressed are you feeling in this moment?	How connected to others and life are you feeling in this moment?
(none) 0 1 2 3 4 5 6 7 8 9 10 (extremely)	(none) 0 1 2 3 4 5 6 7 8 9 10 (extremely)

❧ PROMPT 21 ❧

Anticipatory Savoring

"Anticipatory savoring" is a technique that activates a positive experience in advance—in this case, something meaningful that you now imagine coming out of this morally injurious or morally distressing experience and what you can do to make it more likely to happen.

Imagine your life purpose is calling to you to *do* something—to take some committed action—as one small step in fulfilling that purpose. What is the voice saying?

_____

_____

_____

_____

_____

_____

_____

Now, imagine yourself taking action today in accordance with that voice—maybe even when you set down this book. What are you doing? Maybe that's seeing a new friend that you met because of this situation or spending time with someone you're trying to reconnect with. Imagine the value(s) that are connected to that action. Drop into those feelings, emotions, and sensations and notice what bubbles up. Notice how you're holding pain and hope at the same time. Reflect then record.

_____

_____

_____

_____

_____

_____

_____

_____

_____

_____

_____

Next, imagine yourself taking action in the distant future—something that requires more time and planning; for example, a change in career or going back to school. Imagine the value(s) that are connected to that action. Drop into those feelings, emotions, and sensations and notice what bubbles up. Again, notice how you're holding pain and hope at the same time. Reflect, then record.

Now, imagine yourself using coping strategies. For instance, reaching out to a trusted friend, exercising, or doing mindfulness techniques in case that desired action takes longer than expected or must change for some reason. What are they?

Imagine the value(s) that are connected to those strategies, then drop into those feelings, emotions, and sensations and notice what bubbles up. Notice how the coping strategies help you hold pain and hope at the same time. Reflect, then record.

_____

_____

_____

_____

_____

_____

_____

_____

_____

_____

_____

_____

_____

Finally, reflect on, then record, what this says about your ability to live your purpose or fulfill your calling.

_____

_____

_____

_____

_____

_____

_____

_____

_____

_____

_____

_____

_____

_____

⤲ Post-Writing Check-In ⤳

Take a few moments to sit quietly without looking at what you wrote to transition to the present. Taking a few deep and quiet breaths can help. Mark how you're feeling in this moment on the scales below and jot down any thoughts that arise.

How distressed are you feeling in this moment?	How connected to others and life are you feeling in this moment?
(none) 0 1 2 3 4 5 6 7 8 9 10 (extremely)	(none) 0 1 2 3 4 5 6 7 8 9 10 (extremely)

Use this space to reflect on the writing—how it felt, what was inspiring or challenging.

❧ PROMPT 22 ❧

I Am Here, I Am Ready

Throughout the ages, people have contemplated what it means to live a good life, the moral life—including myself. The most profound response I can think of comes down to one word: *hineni*. *Hineni* is a Hebrew word that means essentially, "I am here, and I am ready." To say "hineni" signals the moment when you situate your own life story within the larger story of life—past, present, and future. And you do this not merely with passive awareness but with active commitment. Hineni embodies an open mind, a willing body, and an engaged soul, even in the face of uncertainty or trepidation. It is a word that stands for light that cannot be drowned out by darkness. No matter how black or bright the hour, *hineni*. No matter how hopeless or hopeful you feel, *hineni*. You may quiver and waver and doubt for a time, but you are ultimately rooted, steadfast, and confident in your true home, *hineni*.

More than referring to being physically present in a specific location, hineni is an existential expression of saying "Yes!" to life. Indeed, it is your response to life when it calls, even if that call is in the form of moral injury or a soul wound. In saying hineni, you are accepting that responsibility by boldly and courageously stepping forward into life "all in" and making all of yourself available to every aspect of life, come what may.

This final prompt will help you to say "Yes!" to life once more.

Imagine yourself standing on a threshold of an open door. In one direction, the landscape of the past is stretched out. Find the spot where your morally injurious or distressing experience happened.

Now, look around you to see who else is there with their own experience of pain. Maybe this is someone close to you, or someone you've only read or heard about. What do you have in common with all these people? Drop into those feelings, emotions, and sensations and notice what bubbles up.

Next, imagine you are talking to each of these people about their morally painful experiences. How does it feel to know you're not alone in your pain, that others *see* you, and that you *see* others? Drop into those feelings, emotions, and sensations and notice what bubbles up.

Reflect on, then record, something new that you see in yourself and the world.

Now, imagine yourself standing on that same threshold of an open door. In the other direction, the landscape of the future is stretched out. Look around you to see who else is there and notice what they're doing—how they are using their life's purpose for good, whether that's for themselves, others, and/or the world. Locate yourself on that landscape and notice what you are doing—how *you* are using your life's purpose for good, whether that's for yourself, others, and/or the world. Drop into those feelings, emotions, and sensations and notice what bubbles up.

Next, imagine you are not only talking to each of these people about their soulful experience of holding remnants of pain but also finding renewed meaning, purpose, and value. How does it feel to see yourself using your own renewed values to serve your life's purpose? Drop into those feelings, emotions, and sensations and notice what bubbles up.

Reflect on, then record, three to five things you must do now to leave that threshold with the open door and step forward, saying, "I am here...and I am ready."

1. _____

2. _____

3. _____

4. _____

5. _____

❧ Post-Writing Check-In ❧

Take a few moments to sit quietly without looking at what you wrote to transition to the present. Taking a few deep and quiet breaths can help. Mark how you're feeling in this moment on the scales below and jot down any thoughts that arise.

How distressed are you feeling in this moment?	How connected to others and life are you feeling in this moment?
(none) 0 1 2 3 4 5 6 7 8 9 10 (extremely)	(none) 0 1 2 3 4 5 6 7 8 9 10 (extremely)

∽ PROMPT 23 ∽

Express Yourself

Trauma practitioners often talk about the importance of the expressive act because it pulls us from our "stuckness" and opens us to new ways of thinking and being. It also leverages our inner resources and gifts and allows us to create something meaningful out of hardship. Research shows self-expression might be one of, if not *the* most important way for people to connect, partner, and grow together.

Self-expression is often something we think of artists or children doing, or what we do when we have the confidence to put ourselves out into the world. But *true* self-expression is the greatest example of the human spirit in action—and it's something that must be done in the face of moral injury or soul wounds—even though it may be hard.

Self-expression, regardless of how or where it manifests, always comes down to three core issues: the choices we make, the things we create, and how we contribute—or what I call the *3Cs of Self-Expression.*

Self-expression is the act of bringing something deep within us into an observable form or a committed action. When faced with moral pain or soul violations, it is not merely making something out of nothing; it is reconnecting with our values to make something specific out of that pain, which is nothing short of transformative.

Imagine the values you identified in the earlier prompt that are most important to you and those that were violated that led to your moral injury or soul wound. Allow them to form in your mind.

Now, imagine the ways you have attempted to avoid or control the consequences of that violation. For instance, shame, guilt, rage, disgust, pulling away from others, shutting down, and self-defeating or self-destructive behavior. Reflect on, then record, what have been the costs of those actions. Drop into those feelings, emotions, and sensations and notice what bubbles up.

Next, imagine those values are beloved old friends whom you haven't seen for some time. You and they are separated by a body of water with a bridge connecting the piece of land where you are now with theirs. The sun is rising in the background and they are waving, calling you to cross. Drop into those feelings, emotions, and sensations and notice what bubbles up.

Now, imagine yourself walking across that bridge to meet those values again after all this time. Again, drop into those feelings, emotions, and sensations and notice what bubbles up. When you get to the other side, imagine those values welcoming you in a friendly embrace, telling you it's great to see you and asking what you want to do—*now*, and *together*.

Reflect on, then record:

Who will you choose to be because of this moral injury or soul wound?

_____

_____

_____

_____

_____

What will you do and create because of this moral injury or soul wound?

_____

_____

_____

_____

_____

What will you contribute to others and the world because of this moral injury or soul wound?

❧ Post-Writing Check-In ❧

Take a few moments to sit quietly without looking at what you wrote to transition to the present. Taking a few deep and quiet breaths can help. Mark how you're feeling in this moment on the scales below and jot down any thoughts that arise.

How distressed are you feeling in this moment?	How connected to others and life are you feeling in this moment?
(none) 0 1 2 3 4 5 6 7 8 9 10 (extremely)	(none) 0 1 2 3 4 5 6 7 8 9 10 (extremely)

_____

_____

_____

_____

_____

_____

_____

_____

_____

_____

⌐ Pause and Appreciate ⌐

Forward into New Life takes nothing less than soul. Like the earlier sections, it asks a lot, but also provides a lot. Take a moment now to congratulate yourself on the important work you've done in Forward into New Life—and all the work you've done in this guided journal.

Final Note from Michele

We've reached the end of our imaginal journey together, at least for this guided journal. To engage in writing about your moral injury or soul wound takes great strength, courage, commitment, and resilience. Please take a moment to acknowledge this.

As you continue your journey of healing moral pain or harm, I encourage you to reflect on the wonderful work you've done here and what you have learned about yourself, what's changed in your life—self-perception, confidence, relationships, personal endeavors, work, peace—and what you feel was most meaningful and important about the process. It's also helpful to reflect on your distress and social connection scores over time and how they changed.

Of course, you do not have to limit yourself to the writing herein. This journal can be used as a launching point for a new writing or journaling practice. People often go back to reconsider or expand on the prompts here; they also use them as inspiration to develop new ones of their own.

Healing from moral trauma and moral adversity means reconciling difficult truths, honoring pain, and transforming ways of thinking and being. It also means being open to both joy and pain, defusing unhelpful thoughts by becoming aware of how emotions, feelings, and sensations are influencing them, and restoring moral integrity by reconnecting with that deepest part of you—your soul. That journey can sometimes be filled with obstacles, particularly as you learn new truths about yourself, others, and the world. Know that setbacks happen, fear returns, newly earned trust becomes shaky, old patterns emerge, and the soul's voice gets harder to hear. If that happens, don't beat yourself up—you're in good company. Just pull out this journal (or get a new journal) and start working through the prompts again. Soon, you'll begin to hear that encouraging voice emerge.

And never forget that change is possible—your courage and commitment make it so.

I am honored to be part of your journey. I wish you healing, hope, happiness, and wholeness as you continue forward in life.

Michele

Acknowledgments

This book would not be possible without the inspiration and support of colleagues, clients, and loved ones.

To Dr. Cindy Shearer, who kept me anchored to the task of creating a coherent, emotionally resonant, safe, and respectful therapeutic intervention (*embodied disclosure therapy*) and who provided penetrating and spirited dialogue for integrating the body into the healing process for moral injury; and to Dr. Jonathan Erickson, whose Imaginal Psychology work sparked my own moral imagination and the *Imaginal Writing* program herein, I am deeply grateful.

To the pioneers in the understanding of moral injury, Jonathan Shay, William Nash, Brian Litz, and Rita Brock; of moral distress, Cynda Rushton; of somatic psychology and trauma, Peter Levine and Bessel van der Kolk; of forgiveness research, Fred Luskin; and of expressive writing, James Pennebaker, thank you. This work stands upon your shoulders.

To my dearest agent and friend, Kimberley Cameron, your tireless support and fierce advocacy leave me without words. You have my endless thanks, appreciation, and admiration.

To my editor, Jed Bickman, who brought this project into being and supported it at every step, I am so very grateful.

To my family—my parents, Rosemary and Charlie; Drew, Sophie, and Seamus—you are my greatest moral good. Love you beyond remainder.

To those who were courageous enough to share their stories with me, especially veterans and service members, healthcare workers, first responders, and law enforcement, who serve society and have suffered and sacrificed much, I thank you and honor your experience. You have taught me so much about moral conflict and the challenges of integrity.

To those who are still struggling to heal the wounds of moral trauma, please know you are not alone.

References

DeMarco, M. 2022. "Embodied Disclosure Therapy: Writing from a Place of Inner Safety and Connection: A Novel Approach for Moral Injury." Doctoral dissertation, California Institute of Integral Studies.

DeMarco, M. 2023. "6 Underestimated Drivers of Well-Being: Research Shows These Psychospiritual Forces May Be Critically Important for Decreasing Risk of Illness and Death and Boosting Overall Health." *Psychology Today*, April 15. https://www.psychologytoday.com/us/blog/soul-console/202304/6-underestimated-drivers-of-well-being.

DeMarco, M. 2024. *Holding onto Air: The Art and Science of Building a Resilient Spirit*. Oakland, CA: Berrett-Koehler.

Evans, W. R., R. D. Walser, K. D. Drescher, and J. K. Farnsworth. 2020. *The Moral Injury Workbook: Acceptance and Commitment Therapy Skills for Moving Beyond Shame, Anger, and Trauma to Reclaim Your Values*. Oakland, CA: New Harbinger Publications.

Gendlin, E. 1978. *Focusing*. New York: Bantam Books.

Levine, P. A.. 2008. *Healing Trauma: A Pioneering Program for Restoring the Wisdom of Your Body*. Louisville, CO: Sounds True.

Levine, P. A. 2010. *In an Unspoken Voice: How the Body Releases Trauma and Restores Goodness*. Berkeley, CA: North Atlantic Books.

Neff, K. 2003. "Self-Compassion: An Alternative Conceptualization of a Healthy Attitude Toward Oneself." *Self and Identity* 2: 85–101. https://doi.org/10.1080/15298860309032.

Pennebaker, J. W., and S. K. Beall. 1986. "Confronting a Traumatic Event: Toward an Understanding of Inhibition and Disease." *Journal of Abnormal Psychology* 95(3): 274–281. https://doi.org/10.1037/0021-843X.95.3.274.

Ruston, C. H. 2017. "Cultivating Moral Resilience." *American Journal of Nursing* 117(2): S11–S15. https://doi.org/10.1097/01.NAJ.0000512205.93596.00.

Michele DeMarco, PhD, is an award-winning writer, and a therapist, clinical ethicist, and trauma researcher specializing in moral injury. She is author of the *Psychology Today* blog *Soul Console*, and one of *Medium*'s Top Writers for Mental Health and Health. Her writing has appeared in national and international publications, including *The New York Times, POLITICO, The Boston Globe, The Daily News, Psychology Today, The Free Press, The War Horse,* and *Medium.* She's been featured as a trauma and spirituality expert for *MindBodyGreen, The Daily News, Integrative Practitioner, Lifehacker,* Bloomberg/WNBP Radio, and Partners HealthCare. She lives in the San Francisco Bay Area.

MORE BOOKS from
NEW HARBINGER PUBLICATIONS

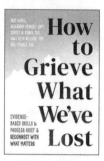